RE/ MODELING YOUTH MINISTRY

"*Remodeling Youth Ministry* addresses significant questions the church faces concerning modern student ministry. I am grateful for Christopher Talbot's work in speaking to these pivotal matters for the sake of the church's mission and the soul of the next generation."

—JUSTIN BUCHANAN, Assistant Professor of Student Ministry, Southwestern Baptist Theological Seminary

"In *Remodeling Youth Ministry*, Chris Talbot discusses a crucial dimension of our twenty-first century church: youth ministry. He provides insightful coaching to both the experienced pastor and the rookie youth minister. Unlike some books on this topic, which take a wrecking ball to the various models of youth ministry, Talbot presents a thoughtful, well-researched, and wonderfully written text suitable for the college and seminary classroom, as well as a group evaluating its youth ministry in the local church. The book's arguments and perspectives are strengthened by the author's use of a wide variety of voices from across our evangelical landscape."

—KEN COLEY, Professor of Christian Education, Southeastern Baptist Theological Seminary, Author of *Teaching for Change* (Randall House)

"*Remodeling Youth Ministry* is a helpful, thoughtful, and compelling guide for the youth worker and parent alike. Balanced and applicable, you will be both challenged and encouraged. Take up and read!"

—BRIAN COSBY, Author of *Giving Up Gimmicks: Reclaiming Youth Ministry from an Entertainment Culture* (P&R)

"New youth ministers are flooded with polarized opinions that either pronounce youth ministry as unbiblical, a weed in the church, or else defend the separation of students from others in the church. Talbot has written a great reconciliation of the extremes in a way that includes contemporary and veteran voices in youth ministry. My hope is that youth ministers will take the time to digest this book and be able to practice a more balanced and intergenerational ministry that assists students in becoming lifelong disciples."

—R. ALLEN JACKSON, Professor of Youth Education and Founder of the Youth Ministry Institute, New Orleans Baptist Theological Seminary

"There is a universal problem in the church with young people leaving the faith. *Remodeling Youth Ministry* is a fantastic resource to aid church leadership in developing a balanced but biblical approach to youth ministry. It's an essential tool for anyone working with young people. Every youth pastor needs to read it."

—MARCOS OSUNA, Student Pastor, Faith Free Will Baptist Church, Goldsboro, North Carolina

"If you're browsing your bookstore and see *Remodeling Youth Ministry* on the shelf, go ahead and put it in your cart. It's a must for the youth minister's library. If I were teaching youth ministry in a formal sense at a college or seminary, or in an informal sense at the local church level, I would use this book. Chris Talbot does a great job of laying those foundational truths that youth ministers should know. His conversational style allows academics and novices alike to understand the best ideas and to implement the best practices for building a healthy youth ministry in your local church. I highly recommend it."

—ALLEN POINTER, Director, Truth and Peace Student Leadership Conference, Pastor, Cofer's Chapel Free Will Baptist, Nashville, Tennessee

"*Remodeling Youth Ministry* is a wonderful read for those entering youth and family ministry. It lays down biblical foundations for how and why we do what we do. For the seasoned YFM, it's a great revisit and refresher to help us re-evaluate the methods and routines we've put into practice. It's a book of substance with spot-on application in the church culture of today."

—JOHNNY SAUNDERS, Youth Pastor, First Free Will Baptist Church of Tampa, Seffner, Florida

"In his efforts to help you design a healthy youth and family ministry, Chris Talbot has constructed a tremendous resource in *Remodeling Youth Ministry* that uniquely combines philosophy, theology, and methodology into one beautifully packaged work. Whether you feel like your ministry needs an overhaul or just a few upgrades, this fantastic book will help you remodel God's way!"

—TOMMY SWINDOL, Lead Pastor, The Donelson Fellowship, Nashville, Tennessee

RE/ MODELING YOUTH MINISTRY

A BIBLICAL BLUEPRINT FOR MINISTERING TO STUDENTS

"O send out thy light and thy truth: let them lead me" (KJV).
– Psalm 43:3a

CHRISTOPHER TALBOT

WELCH COLLEGE
PRESS

Remodeling Youth Ministry: A Biblical Blueprint for Ministering to Students

Published by Welch College Press
1045 Bison Trail, Gallatin, TN 37066
www.welch.edu

Printed in the United States of America

July 2017

First Edition

Cover design: Studio Gearbox
Cover image: Shutterstock
Interior design and typeset: Studio Gearbox
and Katherine Lloyd, The DESK

Because of the dynamic nature of the Internet, any web address or links contained in this publication may have changed since publication and may no longer be valid.

Library of Congress Control Number: 2017944411
ISBN-13: 978-0-9976087-1-7

To my students training and preparing
for youth and family ministry.
May this book help guide your thoughts,
but may God's Word do so infinitely more.

TABLE OF CONTENTS

Foreword . . . . *xi*

Introduction *1*

PART I: **LAYING THE FOUNDATION**

Chapter 1: Is Youth Ministry Biblical? *9*

Chapter 2: The Purpose(s) of Youth Ministry *21*

Chapter 3: Youth Ministry and the Church's Future *33*

PART II: **MAKING RENOVATIONS**

Chapter 4: Being Missional as a Teenager *49*

Chapter 5: Means of Grace and Methodology *63*

Chapter 6: Rethinking Apologetics for Students *79*

Chapter 7: Family Discipleship in Church and Home *93*

PART III: **BUILDING FOR THE FUTURE**

Chapter 8: Preparing for Sustainable Change *109*

Chapter 9: Teaching Teens *123*

Chapter 10: Ministering in an Age of Distraction *137*

Chapter 11: The Gospel of Rest in Ministry *155*

Conclusion *167*

Notes *171*

Bibliography *183*

Acknowledgements *193*

About the Author *195*

FOREWORD

Cameron Cole

The last decade has been a discouraging yet exciting time for youth ministry. Negatively, we have discovered that the youth ministry experiment in the American church has failed to form lasting, church-attending followers of Jesus. Positively, leaders in the field of youth ministry have taken ownership of the problems and have sought answers.

Chris Talbot provides two valuable resources in this conversation: *clarity* and *direction.* He draws from the best research and commentary to frame and analyze the problems facing church youth ministries. He also offers philosophical and concrete direction forward for those looking to lead effective ministries.

In response to the issues, many have lost sight of the purpose of youth ministry and of how to achieve its mission. We need repeated and clear reminding, which Talbot does well: Beneath all of the competing priorities is the central mission of forming a mature faith in young people so that they become lifelong disciples of Jesus Christ.

Yes, we want our young people to change the world. Yes, we want them to take the gospel out into the nations. Yes, we want them to address the pressing issues related to poverty and justice. However, these hopes are as real as unicorns if we do not first teach them what following Jesus faithfully and obediently means. *Remodeling Youth Ministry* will reinforce this fundamental purpose for those leading young people.

Also, young people face numerous and complex spiritual challenges. Technology has brought an onslaught of messages that undermine and subvert the Christian faith. Modern society celebrates and promotes many idols. The essential foundations of church and family have weakened. The challenges can overwhelm those looking to lead young people faithfully to faithfulness.

Still, the solution is simple: the gospel of Jesus Christ. There's no need for cutting-edge methodologies and complicated strategies. Our approach to discipleship-making remains the same today as it did in the early church. We build relationships. We teach God's Word. We proclaim the good news of God's grace for sinners through Christ. We pray. We show people how to follow Christ—all in Christian community. *Remodeling Youth Ministry* will help youth pastors stand in the power of the gospel, the Word of God, and the truth of Christ as they seek to make a lasting difference in the lives of teenagers.

I have dedicated my life to the hope of gospel-centered youth ministry for all young people. My hope is that they will receive the gospel of grace each week by youth pastors teaching the Bible, mentors guiding them into Christian maturity, and parents investing in their spiritual lives.

Can you imagine the impact on the church and our culture if the religious experience for every teenager was like this? It would change the world. *Remodeling Youth Ministry* is another important resource in the mission to uphold Jesus Christ and His gospel as the core of youth ministry.

INTRODUCTION

"Youth is the seed-time of full age—
the molding season in the little space
of human life—the turning point
in the history of man's mind."

- J.C. RYLE[1]

My wife and I recently bought our first home. We were excited to be first-time homeowners. We were also nervous about the work ahead of us. Even though our home was in good condition, we had a list of items that we wanted to ensure was done before moving.

With a minimal budget and plenty of commitment, we began removing the old floor and laying a new one in our living room, painting our kitchen cabinets, changing the electric switches and outlets, replacing old appliances—the list goes on. By the end of it all (home repair is *never* completely finished), we had discovered that remodeling is no easy task.

Home improvement shows make the remodeling process look like a breeze. Even though the participants are sweating, they seem to fix everything within thirty minutes—even less if you don't count the commercials. Unequivocally, this wasn't the case for us. Our remodeling process took much longer, and we had our share of stressful moments. Television made a difficult task seem easier than it was

Our remodeling work wasn't broadcast worthy, but it showed promise. And even with our frustrations, we had one sure hope: The foundation of our house was solid. We could make big mistakes, like rewiring switches incorrectly (which I did), with the confidence that our house would stay standing. We also knew that if we continued to work hard toward the goal we'd set our renovations would look beautiful in the end.

Why do I share this with you? Because it may be time to remodel your current structure of youth ministry with the blueprint of God's Word. I've written this book for that purpose: to lay down a biblical philosophy of youth and family ministry (YFM).

You'll notice that the title of this book utilizes a play on words. Not only does it suggest a *re*model, but it also recognizes that most philosophies of youth ministry have been articulated as *models* of ministry. You may be coming to this book with convictions, preconceived notions, and/or misunderstandings of your own model of youth ministry. Or you may be reading this book with no preconceived notions at all. Instead of reshaping the youth ministry landscape, this book offers some slight corrections and integrations of pre-existing models. Instead of rebuilding the youth ministry house, I propose a remodel.

Why a philosophy, and not a theology, of YFM, you might ask. Warren Benson helpfully notes, "Theology denotes a system of beliefs about God, human nature, the world, the church, and other related topics formulated to enable Christians to comprehend and make sense of their faith. Classically, philosophy was and is engaged in the development of systems for interpreting reality."[2]

Even so, a philosophy of YFM must be built on a theological foundation. While this book will articulate a philosophical paradigm, it aims also to give a theological underpinning. Thus, I want to provide a broad rubric for how to think about YFM.

This book won't answer all of your questions, but I hope it will point you in the right direction. It's not intended to introduce the reader to all that youth ministry offers. Rather, it's a primer. It's intentionally brief, because I know how busy youth pastors can be (see chapter eleven). I didn't want the book to be an inaccessible and daunting tome. As a result, it may skip some topics that the reader believes are important to YFM.

My goal is to get the youth and family minister to think deeply about his ministry, whether he's a novice or a veteran. For too long, YFM has suffered from pragmatic solutions to eternal problems. To echo Dean Borgman, this book is "not so much a how-to-do youth ministry book as a how-to-think-about-youth-and-family-ministry" book.[3]

To quote the Anglican bishop J.C. Ryle, who hoped to encourage the youth of his day in *Thoughts for Young Men*, "Believe me, this world is not a world in which we can do well without thinking, and least of all do well in the matter of our souls."[4] For that reason, I not only want youth ministers to think deeply about their own souls; I also want them to think about the souls of those for whom they're caring.

This book is separated into three parts: (1) Laying the Foundation, (2) Making Renovations, and (3) Building for the Future. In a way, these parts correspond to the past, present, and future of YFM. In the first part, I tackle three primary questions about YFM. Chapter one discusses the crucial question of whether youth ministry is biblical. Chapter two asks why youth ministry exists. Finally, chapter three considers how youth ministry affects "big church." While more questions could be asked, these three questions offer a good start.

Part two deals with shifts that I believe are necessary in our current culture of North American YFM. Some of these moves are more drastic than others. Consistently, though, this section will show the connection between theology and methodology. Chapter four discusses how to make the gospel central in your ministry and how to create a stronger gospel-culture. Chapter five considers how youth groups can take seriously the sufficiency of Scripture. Chapter six tackles the topic of apologetics and suggests a slight course correction in how we should teach it. Chapter seven adds to a chorus of current voices in encouraging the partnership of the church and home.

Finally, part three considers what a successful and sustainable YFM should look like in the future. While I aim to demonstrate practical theology throughout the book, this section is the most practical. Chapter eight, functioning as a segue from part two to part three, recommends helpful steps for creating a sustainable YFM. Chapter nine examines how youth and family ministers can effectively teach teenagers in our current culture with all of its difficulties. Chapter ten surveys the challenges of ministering in a technological age and provides a way forward. Finally, chapter eleven concludes with a message of grace and hope for those in YFM.

You'll also notice "Remodeling Tips" throughout the

chapters. Knowing that we never practice successful ministry on our own, I've included the voices of other youth pastors and leaders who have offered their insights into these various areas.

HOW TO USE THIS BOOK

You can read this book in two ways, either by yourself or in the company of your fellow YFM volunteers and ministers. I believe you will get the most out of this book through interaction with others.

For that reason, I've included discussion questions at the end of each chapter. These serve to get the ball rolling. The chapters themselves, I hope, will encourage inquiry and examination. Often, at least in my own life, the best way to hash out the ideas that I've been thinking about is to share and discuss them with others. Allow this book to prompt discussion and development.

If you're not able to read this book with a group, I recommend that you either keep a journal or write on the pages themselves. Have a conversation with the book as you write. Jot down questions or thoughts; feel free to answer the discussion questions on your own. Chances are that you'll return to those questions and thoughts at a later time to unpack them further.

MY PERSPECTIVE

Finally, I give a short disclaimer. While no one writes and thinks in a vacuum, I want to make you, the reader, aware of my context. Youth ministry books have been written across denominations, philosophies, and theological commitments. I write as an ordained Free Will Baptist minister. I work in a local church as the Pastor of Youth and Family Ministry. This means that I have certain doctrinal beliefs and practices that may differ from others. Though a reader may disagree with me on some finer points of theology, I believe that a wide array of Christians can benefit from this book.

I also write as a college teacher who teaches youth and family ministry. For nine months out of the year, I spend five days a week interacting with college students on the subjects of ministry, theology, and Scripture. They sharpen my mind as much as I hope I sharpen theirs. Therefore, my perspective is informed by both theory and practice.

Further, I believe that the Bible is "written by holy men, inspired by the Holy Spirit," and "God's revealed word to man." It's "a sufficient and infallible rule and guide to salvation and all Christian worship and service. Since the Bible is the Word of God, it's without error in all matters upon which it speaks, whether history, geography, matters relating to science or any other subject."[5] This is a belief that I hold to unabashedly; true youth ministry can't be done outside of this doctrine.

My earnest prayer is that this book will benefit you and your ministry. Though I may not know you personally, I pray that God will use its content in His plan for your ministry; and I pray that you'll rely on Scripture to shape the contours of your methodology. My desire is to see youth ministers and youth ministries across the world glorify God in their practice. Finally, I hope that the following chapters will encourage you to think more deeply about discipling youth.

PART I

LAYING THE FOUNDATION

CHAPTER 1

IS YOUTH MINISTRY BIBLICAL?

"What makes youth ministry distinctive is not its form, but its flock."

– ANDREW ROOT AND KENDA CREASY DEAN[1]

Most of us who've grown up within American evangelicalism have fond memories of youth group. We remember camp messages that focused on our response to the gospel. We remember youth pastors calling on us to take our purity seriously. Whether an all-night lock-in or songs around a campfire, we remember our time in youth group as equal parts fun and spiritual growth. We often look back on our four to six years in a youth ministry and remain thankful—and for good reason!

However, amidst our nostalgia, we often forget to consider our youth group's primary foundation. While youth ministry has quickly become canonized within the evangelical church in the twentieth century,[2] we rarely ask the most important questions about its underpinning. We know that we should share biblical truth in our devotions and messages. We remember to point students to Christ in the good times and bad.

Nevertheless, when we look at what we're doing in the local church, as we focus on teenagers and their spiritual growth, we must consider whether youth ministry is biblical. This is the first and most important question.

THE TENSION

Is youth ministry biblical? No and yes. Recently, Christians have vacillated on this question. Some say that it's a failed experiment, needing to be removed in churches everywhere.

This has been especially true for those connected with the family-integrated church movement. For these believers, youth ministry has failed in its purpose; it's illegitimate and unbiblical. They argue that families hold primary responsibility to disciple their children in spiritual formation, which the church should support. A spokesperson for the National Center for Family-Integrated Churches writes,

> Today's church has created peer dependency. . . . The inherent result of youth groups is that teenagers in the church are focused on their peers, not their parents or their pastors. It's a foreign sociology that leads to immaturity, a greater likelihood of sexual activity, drug experimentation and a rejection of the authority of the Word of God. . . . American Christians are finally waking up to the disconnect between the clear teaching in Scripture in favor of family-integration and the modern-day church's obsession with dividing the family at every turn. Age segregation,

> especially during the tender and impactful teenage years, not only hasn't worked, it's been detrimental. Even worse, it is contrary to the Bible. But the good news is that practices in the churches related to youth groups are changing dramatically. Twenty years ago no one was even asking this question.[3]

Certainly, these statements represent just one side of thinking on youth ministry—one with which not everyone agrees.

Others continue to stand by the concept of youth ministry and, believing it has fostered good, often double down on current youth ministry practices. Those still advocating for youth ministry believe that the concept of family-integration introduces a false dichotomy. One can thoroughly equip parents to disciple their children, they explain, while still operating a ministry geared specifically to the youth. Amidst these varying options, I still believe the answer is both no and yes. While this may sound indecisive, it's true.

A tension prevails in the way that youth ministry is approached and practiced today, which makes all the difference. We all agree that the Bible is the "sufficient and infallible rule and guide to salvation and all Christian worship and service."[4] Thus, we have to examine the intersection between youth ministry and God's Word. We want to ensure that our ministries exhibit the sufficiency of Scripture. A simple no or yes can't adequately answer the question, "Is youth ministry biblical?" It requires more nuance. We must examine the practice—the *how*—of youth ministry in order to substantiate the claim that it's biblical.

Additionally, a second question must be asked: What do we mean by *biblical*? How do we define whether a practice is truly biblically-based? If we're asking whether the contemporary practice of youth ministry is in the Bible, or whether the Bible includes an explicit command to minister to teenagers, or whether the Bible says, "thou shalt have lock-ins," the answer is no (I'm thankful about this especially concerning lock-ins!).

What, then, do we mean by asking whether youth ministry is biblical? Ultimately, we're asking whether a given practice is consistent with the message and mission of Scripture. This goes beyond looking for proof texts but requires the student of Scripture to hold his or her ministry up to the mirror of God's Word. Is it consistent with the Bible? Does it reinforce the focuses of Scripture?

Youth ministry is a practice that helps us accomplish God's commands. Scripture gives us some leeway concerning our method. Because we don't have explicit statements about youth ministry, we must try to "fill in the gaps" with biblical truth. In fact, the Bible should regulate what we do as youth ministers. We want to ensure that we're faithful to Scripture's principles concerning subjects that aren't otherwise clearly addressed in the text. We don't have free license to do simply as we please.

THE ANSWER: NO

We now turn to the question, "Is youth ministry biblical?" Beginning with the negative may seem peculiar, if not completely ludicrous, from someone who teaches and practices youth ministry for a living. If anything, my livelihood depends on youth ministry having at least some scriptural claim.

Nevertheless, the answer is a no, so long as youth ministry remains segregated from the church. Alvin Reid writes, "We are not helping young people grow into maturity when we add to the dichotomy between a weekly time of worship for students and the time when all the people of God gather to worship the holy God and then scatter to live out the mission of God."[5] Unfortunately, this is often the contrast we've chosen.

Many models of youth ministry completely separate the youth from contact with both the older members and younger children of the church. When worship, ministry, and fellowship are segregated, it can send the message that the Christian life is highly customized and individualized, especially for teenagers.

Rather than turning youth ministry into a para-church organization, the youth leader should focus on the integrative, spiritual function of teenagers within the local church. Certainly, para-church organizations offer great benefits to the church. However, Christ has chosen the local church, and not para-church organizations, to advance His kingdom on earth (Acts 1:3; 28:31). For that reason, youth ministry is unbiblical so long as it works apart from the church in its discipleship of teenage Christians.

In addition, such segregation creates unbiblical youth. We often hear things like, "They need their own space and their own activities." However, consider the qualities that the Bible commands the church to be: communal, confessional, and purposeful.[6] Our identity is in Christ alone.[7]

Insofar as teenagers belong to the church—and they do—they should also reflect these characteristics. Teenagers, like all people, have a deep, abiding desire or yearning for something bigger, something better—what some have referred to as *Sehnsucht*.[8] The church alone offers the remedy to this longing.

Those youth ministries that successfully produce disciple-teenagers are, according to Kenda Creasy Dean, author of *Almost Christian*, a part of congregations that "view young people, not as moralistic do-gooders, but as Christ's representatives in the world."[9] Allowing youth ministry to stay interwoven with the church helps teenagers to satisfy their deepest questions and to recognize their call as Christian disciples.

THE ANSWER: YES

At the same time, we might say that youth ministry *is* biblical. Scripture is full of statements about our ministry to youth. The Bible explains that youth are a blessing (Genesis 3:5; 48:9; Psalm 128:1-4) and are vital to God's covenant work in humanity (Genesis 12-13). Christ Himself blessed youth (Matthew 19:13-15), pointed to youth as an illustration of humility (Mark 9:42-48), and gravely warned any who might cause a youth to stumble (Luke 17:1-2).

Even more, Scripture consistently accounts the spiritual endeavors of youth. Many believe that David was a teenager when he faced Goliath, or that Joseph was seventeen at the beginning of his story. Jeremiah thought that he was too young to be a prophet (Jeremiah 1:6), and Timothy was exhorted as a youth (2 Timothy 2:22).[10] Yet the label *youth* had far less bearing then than it does today. It was used simply to describe the youth's age and didn't refer to their behavior; in fact, teenagers were expected to behave like adults.[11]

What does the Bible say about ministry to youth? Deuteronomy 6:7-9 charges parents to teach the commandments to their children. Ephesians 6:1 encourages children, albeit briefly, to obey their parents. One passage admonishes parents directly to minister to youth; the other admonishes youth directly to follow a biblical commandment.

What we might easily overlook in both of these passages is this: They are both given in the context of the faith community, the first in the assembly of the Israelites and the second to the church in Ephesus.[12] Both admonitions occur in the context of God's people. This means that youth should never separate from the local community of faith.

The discipleship of our youth, then, occurs in our homes and churches. What does that mean for our understanding of the body of Christ? In 1 Corinthians 12:12-26, Paul, though not directly speaking to youth, highlights the diversity found within the unified body of Christ. Agreeing with John's picture of the church in Revelation 7:9, Paul believes that it should be made up of "every tribe and tongue." Thus, to have a biblical representation of the church today is to have a wide array of diversity and to minister in light of that diversity.

Writing for the Fuller Youth Institute, Mike Kipp states that whether youth ministry is biblical depends on our goal of youth ministry.[13] Youth ministry "mission statements" can range anywhere from "saving teens" to "promoting purity." Youth ministry, as Kipp argues, should ultimately exist "to integrate young people into the body and mission of Jesus Christ."[14] As a result, youth ministry should be church-centric, since that's how Scripture conceives of the community of God's people.

As one writer formulated, the biblical mandate for youth ministry should move from the home to the church to mentorship: "Begin religious instruction in the family home as spiritual practices, add knowledge through the larger community of faith, and provide mentoring from key spiritual leaders for specific practices and duties."[15] This defines youth ministry not as a ghettoized ministry of the church but as holistic and deeply interwoven in the life of the local church.

REMODELING TIP

Many people have opinions about me. But no one's is as important as that of my eleven-year-old daughter. That's why Ellie's recent words felt like a Ginsu knife cutting through the tennis shoe of my heart (if you haven't seen that infomercial, it's time to search).

One of her friends was moving to Georgia. The girl's father, who'd been an associate pastor for years, had taken a lead ministry position. This inspired her inquisitive little mind to ask me, "Dad, are you ever going to be a real pastor?"

I've been pastoring for more than two of her lifetimes. I'm older than my lead pastor. I'm baptizing the children of children that I baptized early in my ministry, but all that experience was reduced to ashes by ten words from an eleven-year-old girl.

If you ever want to boil something "down to the low gravy," as we say in the South, explain it to an eleven-year-old. It's better than writing a hundred pages in a Philosophy of Youth Ministry course.

I explained to Ellie that my job is making disciples for Christ, just like "real" pastors do. And yes, I made angry air quotes with my fingers when I said the word *real*.

I love the word *pastor*. It captures so many wonderful parts of what I'm blessed to do. Pastoring is giving an exhausted parent tools to help his or her terrified daughter sleep at night. It's trying to figure out how to verbalize how you're ecstatic to welcome the student who leads the homosexual club at your local high school to your youth group and yet remaining faithful to God's Word.

Leading people to Christ and helping them find their God-ordained place of ministry: You can't get any more real than that.

- Jon Forrest, Pastor to Students and Families, Bethel Free Will Baptist Church, Ashland City, Tennessee

---

CONCLUSION

We should love youth ministry. But we should love the church more. While this may seem counter-intuitive, the reason that we should love the church more is because we love our youth. If we love the youth, then we desire that they be integrated into that larger community of faith to be discipled, instructed, loved, and held accountable. For the Christian, this occurs only in the body of Christ.

We do this by not simply ministering to students but also ministering with students. Be intentional about making space for students to be in the church choir, serve as ushers, read Scripture during worship, and even teach. Connect your students as much to the church as possible, giving them avenues to minister and to be ministered to. In no way does this mean that we must jettison youth ministry. However, it does mean that we might have to change the way we do youth ministry. We can continue to minister directly and specifically to teenagers, but our purposes must be aligned with the purposes of the church ordained by God in Scripture.

Alvin Reid states, "The church in America stands at a crossroads, and student ministry sits right in the center of the intersection."[16] As Christians, we want to be deeply biblical. As youth pastors, let us begin with the Bible as our foundation, and let it saturate everything we do. Let's hold our youth ministries up to the mirror of Scripture and see the Bible evident in all that we do.

Discussion Questions

1. What kind of ministry practices would make youth ministry unbiblical?
2. How has the history of the church generally understood its ministry to youth?
3. What forms of inclusion, in the practice of the church, can help a youth ministry become more biblical?
4. What role does the family have in making youth ministry a biblical institution?
5. How else might you make a biblical basis for youth ministry?
6. What elements of the local church does youth ministry need to reflect consistently?

Helpful Resources

Dave Keehn, "Biblical Mandate for Youth Ministry (Part 3): Youth Ministry in the New Testament," *The Good Book Blog*, March 5, 2012; http://www.thegoodbookblog.com

/2012/mar/05/biblical-mandate-for-youth-ministry-part-3-youth-m/; accessed January 9, 2015; Internet.

Paul G. Kelly, "A Theology of Youth," *Journal for Baptist Theology and Ministry*, vol. 13, no. 1 (Spring 2016).

Mike Kipp, "Is 'Youth Ministry' in the Bible? Researching the Scripture Behind Youth and Family Ministry," *Fuller Youth Institute*, July 30, 2012; http://fulleryouthinstitute.org/articles/is-youth-ministry-in-the-bible; accessed January 9, 2015; Internet.

Mike McGarry, "Is Youth Ministry Really New to the Church?" *Rooted Ministry*, September 13, 2015; https://www.rootedministry.com/blog/is-youth-ministry-really-new-to-the-church/; accessed November 25, 2016; Internet.

CHAPTER 2

THE PURPOSE(S) OF YOUTH MINISTRY

"Effective youth ministry happens when a very consistent set of factors is put in place, and it flounders when those factors are absent."

– MARK DeVRIES[1]

In those early months of my first full-time youth ministry position, I was green but eager and excited to minister to students and their families. I found out quickly that others were just as eager as I was to see the youth ministry grow.

Before long, though, some finer points of disagreement emerged. While I never experienced big disputes, I could sense the competing perspectives. Underneath well-meaning exhortations were competing philosophies of ministry. Volunteers and parents that I respect deeply to this day had ideas, wisdom, opinions, and suggestions on what youth ministry should do and where it should go. They cared deeply for our teenagers and wanted to see them grow spiritually. Yet we differed on what that looked like.

In those early days of youth ministry, I thought through the different models that I was hearing from others. I wanted to know why so many well-meaning Christians could have such a diversity of opinion on how we minister to youth. In the end, the answer, in part, was that we all had different understandings on the purpose of youth ministry. In other words, we disagreed on why youth ministry exists.

Thinking back to chapter one, we've answered whether youth ministry is biblical. That is the most vital question, and it's foundational to our ministry practice. While we've already touched on this secondary question of the purposes of youth ministry, we will consider it more fully here. The answer to this question determines whether it's biblical. Youth ministry professionals largely agree on the biblical basis and value of youth ministry. However, they often disagree on youth ministry's purpose or its overarching model.[2]

Although we've laid the foundation on Scripture, we want to begin building upwards. We want to make our philosophy of ministry strong and fortified. We want to find out what the purpose in ministering to youth should be.

MYRIAD POSSIBILITIES

There is no shortage of youth ministry models. Take a look at the youth ministry section of your local Christian bookstore to see the wide array of models that different youth ministry professionals support. From Mark DeVries's *Family-Based Youth Ministry* to Doug Fields's *Purpose-Driven Youth Ministry* to Rick Lawrence's *Jesus-Centered Youth Ministry,* the options are endless.[3]

For the novice youth worker, the virtual smorgasbord of ministry models can be overwhelming. Which one should I pick? Which one is the best for my students? Which one is the most biblical? While this chapter may not answer all of those questions fully, I hope it will equip you to evaluate better your resources and practices that orient the purpose of your ministry.

Too often, youth pastors pick the model they believe will provide the best, and quickest, results. Yet this turns youth ministry into nothing more than a technology, used to increase capital (see chapter ten).[4] We end up picking a ministry model on what it can do for us, rather than how well it mirrors Scripture. Mark DeVries notes, "Most churches have chosen to do youth ministry with a model best described as gambling."[5] We put ourselves, and more so our students, at risk by giving into the success syndrome.[6]

The quickest and most pragmatic model isn't always the most sustainable. Even more, it is rarely the most biblical. We can quickly lose sight of why we're ministering. Ministry isn't about making notches on our baptism belt, but it's instead about caring for students the way that Christ cares for us (Matthew 25:31-46). DeVries continues, "Effective youth ministry happens when a very consistent set of factors is put in place, and it flounders when those factors are absent."[7] I would argue that those consistent factors need to be articulated in the purpose of youth ministry.

In a discipline as diverse as youth ministry, how are you to find and implement a purpose? Some may recommend that you begin with a vision statement or by "casting a vision." The ideas of perpetuating a vision for ministry may sound foreign. This often includes what you see your youth ministry doing in the next one, five, or ten years, and then articulating it for your workers, volunteers, and students.

I understand the principle at work here, and I wouldn't entirely disagree with the practice. However, I would encourage youth ministers to pause and think on the words of Dietrich Bonhoeffer, which are abrasive yet helpful:

> God hates visionary dreaming; it makes the dreamer proud and pretentious. The man who fashions a visionary ideal of community demands that it be realized by God, by others, and by himself. He enters the community of Christians with his demands, sets up his own law, and judges the brethren and God Himself accordingly. He stands adamant, a living reproach to all others in the circle of brethren. He acts as if he is the creator of the Christian community, as if his dream binds men together. When things do not go his way, he calls the effort a failure. When his ideal picture is destroyed, he sees the community going to smash. So he becomes, first the accuser of his brethren, then an accuser of God, and finally the despairing accuser of himself.[8]

Bonhoeffer's words can be difficult for us to hear in our modern ministries. Before you reject the quotation and close this book, think about the truth of this statement. Bonhoeffer is not saying that God hates purpose in ministry, but rather that a sovereign God is displeased when we hijack ministry to serve our own purposes.

If we "cast a vision" (whatever that means), implementing our own ideas and aspirations, we've robbed the ministry of God's glory. The worst thing that we can do, regarding purpose in ministry, is to follow our own desires and preferences. Instead, our purposes should be thoroughly rooted in Scripture and Christian practice; sometimes this may even mean casting a vision. How should we envision the purpose of our ministry?

SINGULAR IN FOCUS

Amidst myriad ministry models, the gospel should be youth leaders' singular purpose—as Mark 1:1 puts it, "the gospel of Jesus Christ, the Son of God." Chap Clark notes, "Today's youth ministry is in desperate need of a theological, psychosocial, and ecological grounding."[9] By the *gospel*, I don't mean only evangelism or apologetics but rather the entirety of the good news of Jesus Christ, which radically transforms every sphere of the believer's life.

This good news results in salvations, which begin with conversion, the repentance from sin, and a trust in Christ as our Lord. It doesn't stop there, though. It's not simply the entrance to Christianity; it's the entirety of the Christian life. Through the gospel, we're united with Christ, which drastically renews and reshapes our lives. Gospel transformation in our own lives and in the lives of our students is our purpose.

Duffy Robbins writes, "Youth ministry without theology—divorced from deep intimacy and communion with God—is little more than a vulgarity."[10] I agree with Robbins (and others) that youth ministry is primarily a theological exercise.[11] This may sound overly cerebral, but before reacting too strongly, think again on Robbins's quotation. Doing youth ministry theologically is not some form of heady practice. Often, people may hear the word *theology* and think that it is too big, impractical, or divisive.[12]

On the contrary, theology is wonderful; it's for all of life, and it brings deep unity among believers. Theology isn't memorizing a list of complicated words. Theology is, as Robbins states, "soul work."[13] It's "deep intimacy and communion with God."[14] Theology is all about "knowing God," as J. I. Packer puts it.[15] As youth ministers, our theology, or our knowledge of God, should inform every aspect of our ministry. Of course, this will directly inform our purpose.

This chapter (and book) is built on a very important presupposition: Theology drives methodology.[16] What we think and know about God affects our ministry practice. What God tells us about others and ourselves affects how we care for people. Certainly, we want to have the mind of Christ (1 Corinthians 2:16) and apply that form of thinking to our Christian life and ministry (Romans 12:1-2). As Dean Borgman notes, "We all need reminders that practical ministry and practical theology flow from God and are intricately connected to each other."[17] Our purpose is rooted in the gospel and theologically informed.

Therefore, I argue that the singular purpose for youth ministry can be found in Colossians 1:24-29:

> Now I rejoice in my sufferings for your sake, and in my flesh I am filling up what is lacking in Christ's afflictions

> for the sake of his body, that is, the church, of which I became a minister according to the stewardship from God that was given to me for you, to make the word of God fully known, the mystery hidden for ages and generations but now revealed to his saints. To them God chose to make known how great among the Gentiles are the riches of the glory of this mystery, which is Christ in you, the hope of glory. *Him we proclaim, warning everyone and teaching everyone with all wisdom, that we may present everyone mature in Christ.* For this I toil, struggling with all his energy that he powerfully works within me.[18]

The purpose of youth ministry is to present young believers mature in Christ through the gospel. After all, what can the church—and therefore youth ministry—offer students that this world can't? Wayne Rice writes, "The only thing that sets the church apart from any other humanitarian organization is Jesus Christ and what he accomplished for us on the cross."[19] Christ's finished work on the cross sets apart those who put their faith in Him. The gospel, and all that it provides, sets our ministries apart from everything else in which our students participate.

Don't be mistaken. Helping young believers achieve gospel maturity is no easy task. What I'm proposing is not a silver-bullet solution for ministry—far from it. But in seeking to achieve this purpose, we'll echo Paul; we'll struggle with all our energy as Christ, through His Spirit, works within us (Colossians 1:29). We'll feel the weight of responsibility to which God has called us, toiling endlessly as we care for the students with whom God has charged us.

God has given us our flock, no matter how awkward, depraved, silly, or ashamed they may be, to steward carefully and graciously. We should treat them as whole people created by God in need of a Savior and the continual work of the Spirit.

Unlike in other forms of ministry, youth ministers deal with students who are in an ever-changing landscape, not only physically but also psychologically, spiritually, and culturally. We should seek to help students grow in their faith in this tumultuous time. While everything around our students is changing, we must root ourselves deeply in the truth of Scripture and help them to do likewise. Thus, as our ministries are focusing on helping students mature in their faith, we must show them how to remain steadfast in a relentless and shifting world. Because of that, some changes may need to be made.

REMODELING TIP

I joined the youth ministry scene from an unlikely avenue. To say that God's grace has been present is a great understatement. I've tried to consider how a graduating senior class should look: If students were to love God's Word, listen to His voice, and live obedient lives to His glory, what characteristics should be present in their lives? I simply worked backwards from there.

I've realized that I don't need to have all the answers to all the problems my students face. I just need constantly to point them to the one who does. I try to push my students to talk to the Lord, read His Word, and listen for what He says.

Several years ago I asked one of the guys in my small group to read a chapter of Scripture out loud for the group. I don't remember what the chapter was or even what we were discussing. All I remember is how long it took him to read and how embarrassed I was for him. No one understood a word as he mumbled and fumbled his way through.

The awkwardness turned my face blood red; I wanted somehow to cut it short. "I shouldn't have asked him to read the whole chapter! Or at least, I should've picked a shorter one!" I thought. That's when I realized that may have been one of the first times he'd ever read Scripture out loud. We may not have understood what he read, but God's Word is alive and transformational, and He began a work that night.

Fast-forward to this past winter. That same guy told me in casual conversation that he reads God's Word daily in His personal devotions. Just a few weeks ago, as he walked across the stage in his cap and gown, I heard, as his name was read off, that one of his focuses in college will be missions!

No one would have expected that—except a youth pastor who kept pushing him to read God's Word and to listen for God's response, reminding him of God's answer during those times of prayer and encouraging him to love God's Word more and more.

Indeed, youth ministry is an important part of God's work. Although I never expected to be in this work, I'm glad I am. To God be the glory.

- Allen Hood, Pastor of Student Ministries, Rejoice Church, Owasso, Oklahoma

---

SO WHAT?

If maturity in the gospel is the focus of youth ministry, some implications follow. We can't simply subscribe to a particular purpose or youth ministry model and continue working the way we've always done it. Our purpose changes our practice. You must analyze this purpose for your own youth ministry and see what might need to change. Although what follows isn't exhaustive, it's a helpful starting point in one's local church.

First, we must realize that maturity, the process of sanctification, is a long process; no short cuts will achieve it. It's easy for us to think that there's a silver bullet to solve our ministerial difficulties. Silver bullets, though, aren't real and have never solved the struggle of ministry. A silver-bullet, short-cut-mentality has only ever killed the ministries whose leaders sought to use them.

Instead, you should allow the long process of God's work to inform your youth ministry practice. As a leader or volunteer, you're called to be faithful to the ministry that God has given you. You're going to be tempted in all sorts of different ways to buy into the temptation of pragmatism and ease. Forget about it. To mature, to become more like Christ, takes a long time, both for you and for others. Model and teach it in front of your students. Allow them to learn both visually and verbally.

Second, eliminate any methodologies, structures, and practices that hinder the maturation process. This is a helpful rubric, especially for those who may be just beginning in a youth ministry position. This will require a certain level of self-awareness and honesty. It may also be difficult, if it requires eliminating programs that you yourself enjoy or that have been around for a long time but don't serve the ultimate purpose.

We must remember the end goal: to present students mature in Christ. If something doesn't follow the principles of Scripture or help achieve your biblical purpose, then it's just taking up space or even hindering your biblical purpose.

Third, every member should be equipped and engaged in service for Christ. This is what the Bible calls spiritual gifts (Romans 12:6-8; 1 Corinthians 12:8-10, 28-30; Ephesians 4:11). Too often, and unintentionally, we emphasize only those gifts that may present a person as artistic or articulate.

Yet the Bible tells us that all believers are equipped for Christian service (1 Peter 4:10). This means, as your students put their faith in the gospel and experience the indwelling of the Spirit, they'll be equipped in service for Christ's Kingdom. Your responsibility is to give them opportunities to use those gifts. Give them opportunities to be involved in the local church, in outreach events, or day-to-day ministry. We want to help students mature not only in their thinking but also in their Christian living.

Discussion Questions

1. What is the most important purpose of youth ministry?
2. How does theology help rather than hinder formulating a purpose for youth ministry?
3. What level of spiritual maturity can the average teenager achieve today?
4. What are some other practical applications for the singular purpose mentioned in this chapter?
5. How does the gospel transform our purpose(s)?
6. What are some ways your theology can drive your methodology?

Helpful Resources

Chap Clark, ed., *Youth Ministry in the 21st Century: Five Views* (Grand Rapids, Mich.: Baker Academic, 2015).

Cameron Cole and Jon Nielson, eds., *Gospel-Centered Youth Ministry: A Practical Guide* (Wheaton, Ill.: Crossway, 2016).

Richard R. Dunn and Mark H. Senter III, eds., *Reaching a Generation for Christ: A Comprehensive Guide to Youth Ministry* (Chicago: Moody, 1997).

Duffy Robbins, *This Way to Youth Ministry: An Introduction to the Adventure* (El Cajon, Calif.: Youth Specialties Academic, 2004).

Andrew Root and Kenda Creasy Dean, *The Theological Turn in Youth Ministry* (Downers Grove, Ill.: Intervarsity, 2011).

Mark H. Senter III, Wesley Black, Chap Clark, and Malan Nel, *Four Views on Youth Ministry: Inclusive Congregational, Preparatory, Missional, Strategic* (El Cajon, Calif.: Youth Specialties Academic, 2001).

CHAPTER 3

YOUTH MINISTRY AND THE CHURCH'S FUTURE

"If ever the church is to flourish again, one must begin by instructing the young."

- MARTIN LUTHER[1]

What's the one staple that you can find in virtually every youth group across America? You're right: the (overly) pre-owned couch. Whether you're in Idaho or Illinois, California or Connecticut, the signature of any well-christened youth room is an old couch.

You can imagine the stories behind the acquisition of these couches. For some, the youth director, due to his low budget (another perennial feature), bought a couch from the local thrift store. Others were procured from a caring church member, looking to "bless" the youth ministry with a piece of furniture.

Many of us have a picture of our beloved youth group couch etched into our minds. More so, we have fond memories of what that couch represented. Those who were diligent to be early to youth group found their favored spot (not to be confused with James 2:1-3) on the couch. Others would come in later, only to squeeze themselves between friends, obviously surpassing the maximum occupancy.

The couches were always well worn, with holes everywhere and soda stains galore. They weren't particularly comfy, and they certainly weren't pretty, but they stood for something more: community. We knew that we were part of something bigger than ourselves when we entered the youth room and took our spot on that dirty, old couch. We were with people who cared for us and loved us—and that makes our memories of that dismal timeworn couch all the fonder.

"Why are we discussing couches?" you may ask. It's because there is a deep formative aspect of youth ministry that endures throughout our entire lives. When we think about that couch, we think about the influence that youth ministry has had on our lives. What we did, saw, and experienced in our foundational years in church has shaped us in profound ways.

Furthermore, what we do in youth ministry isn't formative just to us; it reaches the entire church. As we continue to think about the foundation of youth ministry, we have to think not only about the biblical nature of youth ministry (chapter one) or its present purpose (chapter two), but also about how it affects the future of church and Christian practice.

For that reason, this chapter will explore the impact that popular youth ministry has had on our understanding of contemporary ecclesiology (the doctrine of the church), as well as the continued effect that our youth ministry can have on future Christian generations.

YOUTH MINISTRY YESTERDAY, "BIG CHURCH" TODAY

If you've been in youth ministry for a short amount of time, you may have heard dialogue about what Stuart Bond called the "One-Eared Mickey Mouse."[2] Bond argued that we have ostracized youth to a type of ghetto in the church, separating them from the life of the church as a whole.

Just like a Mickey Mouse head with one ear, youth ministry was connected to the church but only by a thin line. This made youth ministry more of a para-church organization than a local church ministry, something that came alongside the church rather than being involved in the church itself. You might think, as a result, that youth ministry forfeited its ability to affect change in the church.

Surprisingly, the opposite has proved true. Youth ministry has had a profound impact on the church's development. In fact, I propose that *what was done in much youth ministry in recent decades is now becoming normative for the church as a whole.* Likewise, what is being done in youth ministry today will become normative for the church in decades to come. For us to prove this thesis, we'll need to examine the evidence. This will require that we survey the practices in American evangelicalism within the past century.

A helpful case study for this thesis is Bill Hybels, with his experience both in youth ministry and later as a senior pastor. Thomas Bergler points out in *The Juvenilization of American Christianity*, "In subsequent decades, seeker-service pioneers like Bill Hybels and Rick Warren would use the same [youth ministry] techniques to attract Baby Boomer adults to church. . . . The white evangelical churches that are growing the fastest in America are the ones that look the most like the successful youth ministries" of the last generation.[3]

In other words, Bergler argues that many of the attractional church leaders of today are using the same ministry practices that they established in youth ministry years ago. What attracted a certain generation into youth ministry in their adolescence is now being used again to bring them into "big church."

G. A. Pritchard, writing about Hybels's Willow Creek Community Church, states, "Virtually all the church's work has remained firmly in the hands of people who shared the common experience of the youth group."[4] Not only was Hybels using his experience in youth ministry, but those who helped in his youth group also led the church. Clearly, Hybels's background in youth ministry was and is deeply tied to Willow Creek's whole church practice.

While this idea may sound outlandish at first, this thesis has rung true time and time again. "Many visible leaders of today's 'alternative' congregations—church movements where pastors intentionally refashion styles of worship, patterns of polity, and forms of nurture to attract Baby Boomers and/or their progeny—admit strong roots in youth ministry," explain Andrew Root and Kenda Creasy Dean in *The Theological Turn in Youth Ministry*. "A quick scan through their proliferating publications show that, by and large, these leaders simply adapted the visions, methods, and rhetoric of youth ministry to address the adults these youth inevitably became."[5]

Once again, this is probably most explicitly seen in the ministry of Hybels. He has been among the most open about utilizing youth ministry practices for the full church. While he was pioneering a successful youth ministry called Son City at South Park Church in Park Ridge, Illinois, the leadership of the church asked him to replicate the same ministry—only for adults.[6] Thus, Hybels's church ministry was born.

Suffice it to say, youth programs from years before are now shaping the way in which we worship together corporately, across all generations. As a generation has transitioned from one ministry of the church to another, the ministry model has transitioned with them. Leaders are unashamed to admit that they often learned their "tools of the trade" in youth ministry.

In some ways, this may not be a negative influence. The practice has brought numerical growth and a sense of youthful vitality to many who have embraced it. However, what concerns me is not so much the evangelistic emphasis, which is something I believe youth ministry has often gotten right. Rather, it's those other consequences that this paradigm shift has induced. Before moving the entire congregation to the youth room, let's take a step back and try to survey the far reach of this idea.[7]

REMODELING TIP

I began serving at Friendship Free Will Baptist Church at age twenty when I was a sophomore at Welch College. I was trying to figure out a biblical philosophy of youth ministry (I still am), as well as the best way for me to grow our youth group biblically and numerically. Thinking of the church's future, I wanted to build our youth ministry on something that would last long after my students' teenage years. I hoped to see them active in the local church for years to come (I still do).

With that goal in mind, I have structured my youth ministry in a way that parallels the church's ministry. Our youth classes and services closely resemble "big church" services. I try to lead them in singing the Word, giving tithes and offerings, and listening to the preached Word on an age-appropriate level. I don't want the youth unequipped; I want them to understand the purposes behind the adult service structure when they're no longer in the youth group.

Yes, young people are the leaders of the church of tomorrow. However, they're not simply tomorrow's leaders; they're also today's leaders. As a result, we should involve them in "big church." This will allow them to see firsthand the way adults worship together in the corporate setting, to observe Christian worship modeled by mature believers, and to participate in worship with the whole church body.

By doing these things, I hope to cultivate an awe of and desire for biblical corporate worship among our youth so that, when they are the leaders of the future church, they can lead us well.

- Zach Vickery, Associate and Youth Pastor, Friendship Free Will Baptist Church, Ashland City, Tennessee

---

REDRAWING THE ECCLESIAL MAP

What causes me some trepidation is the impact that youth ministry has had and will have on practical ecclesiology. Ecclesiology is the doctrine of the church—what God has told us about His bride (Ephesians 5:25-27; Revelation 19:7-9), and what we should do in response.

My concern is that the tributary of youth ministry is having a far greater impact on the great river of the church than we initially suspected. What we intentionally, and more often unintentionally, implement and practice within student ministry is formulating our thoughts on what the church should do and be in the future. Should this be the case?

Kenda Creasy Dean, Professor of Youth, Church, and Culture at Princeton Theological Seminary, quoted that a 1994 report to the Lilly Endowment stated, "What has become clear . . . is that youth ministry is ultimately about something much more than youth ministry. . . . These [Christian youth] movements are redrawing the ecclesial map of the United States."[8] This is an astounding observation. We're not just borrowing from youth ministry for church today; youth ministry is changing the way we think about the church from here forward. Youth ministry has a deep influence, and we need to take notice.

As one source notes, "In every corner of the globe, youth ministry acts as the church's 'research and development' department."[9] This observation really gets to the root of the issue. Youth ministry has functioned for a long time as the "test site" for practical ecclesiology. In many ways, it's ceased to be real ministry to real people but rather a place to see if different methods and programs work. Before seeing how something might fare in the church, the thinking goes, let's try it in a youth ministry setting first. Of course, our youth are more than ecclesial lab rats.

One could argue that modern-day youth ministry was created to solve a problem. Regrettably, that fix-it mentality has trickled into the church. Chap Clark notes, "Youth ministry as practiced in North America both in the church and in para-church ministries grew out of a desire to correct what many saw as the church's dangerous neglect of young people."[10]

Of course, this stands in contrast to the way that youth ministry has largely been done throughout church history; historically, it's had more of a focus on catechesis.[11] Root goes a step further, saying that modern youth ministry is a technology:

> American youth ministry, since its inception in the mid-twentieth century, has been engendered with a technological mind-set; North American youth ministry has been a *technology*. It is no surprise that the age of the technological—the age in which American society was gripped by a consumptive drive for the new and better (that only a technological society could provide)—was the age of contemporary American youth ministry's beginnings. . . . Youth ministry was created as a technology, needed to solve the problem of adolescent religious apathy, and thus exited for functional growth, as all technologies do. . . . As technology created to functionally solve . . . problems, youth ministry could only be judged by its increased capital. . . . This technological ethos has begun to feel like a noose around the neck of youth workers.[12]

Root's point has immediate implications for the purpose of youth ministry. If youth ministry exists only to deal with functional problems, then its purpose will reflect this perspective.

Numerous problems emerge from this progression. Most notably, when we copy and paste popular youth ministry practices into the entire church, invariably it will lead to a lack of maturity among our congregants. Furthermore, we'll fail to establish our ecclesiology in a biblical-historic foundation but rather in the amorphous entity we call youth culture.

If pastors are borrowing from youth ministry today and will inevitably derive some elements from youth ministry in the future, what needs to be done? Mark H. Senter III writes,

> The bad news is that youth ministry in the twentieth century has shaped the Protestant church of the twenty-first century. Many of the flaws of youth ministry in the twentieth century are showing up in a wide variety of churches in the twenty-first century. Doctrinally thin, ethically tolerant, and consumer-oriented, many churches have lost their passion for the hard sayings of the Christian gospel.[13]

Youth ministries, and possibly youth themselves, are helping guide the ecclesial ship. Inherent in this is the influence of youth culture upon ecclesiology. This harkens back to our discussion on theology. The guiding principle for our church practice should be God's special revelation contained in Christian Scripture. This isn't because youth are incapable, but because Scripture is God's very word to us—our ultimate guide. If we don't look to Scripture, we'll find ourselves on a slippery slope, always searching for something else to guide our methods and ministry.

Notre Dame Sociologist Christian Smith writes, "American culture has little to pass on to American youth with which they can navigate life beyond their experiences of their own subjective desires and feelings—on which alone it is not possible to build good lives."[14] The Bible is the only standard by which we can properly shape our youth ministries and our churches.

SO WHAT DO WE DO?

Seeing the progression and impact of current trends, we can agree with Root and Dean: "Youth ministry is no longer about youth."[15] We must teach our pastors and ourselves about the relationship between youth culture and ecclesiology. This may include teaching our volunteers and staff about the connection between youth ministry and the whole church. We must explain that our practices aren't isolated to the youth room. In the same way that our dilemma has present-future implications, we must exhort our ministers to apply wisdom in both of these areas, using discretion and discernment as they observe new ministry practices.

Today, pastors must continue to seek biblical wisdom when discerning how to reform church practices. Instead of simply keeping the same practices that the past generation used in teen ministry, pastors should place a large emphasis on spiritual maturity. Focusing on this will help the pastor lead his people in their own sanctification.

Likewise, youth pastors should remember the power they hold. Too often, we think the youth pastor is a young maverick, existing as a ministry "catch-all." To the contrary, the youth pastor holds much weight and responsibility. The practices that youth pastors cultivate and promote will not only form students spiritually now, but they will also leave a legacy, affecting students for generations. The youth pastor carries a large burden. This is all the more reason for youth pastors to build on scriptural means of grace (an idea we'll explore later).

Although some aspects of youth ministry will come and go, other elements and practices will form students in deep ways, shaping their entire lives. As one author put it, "Youth ministry is the back door for renewing the church and reorienting her toward its mission—and youth ministry changes more than you know."[16]

Our heart for the gospel, zeal for mission, concern for the oppressed, and love for our Christian brothers and sisters can often be traced to behaviors we learned from Scripture in youth group. Let's not underestimate the power of Scripture in the life of youth and youth ministry.

"One of the most important lessons of our history is that every youth ministry path both closes down some possibilities and opens up new opportunities to renew the church," explains Thomas Bergler. "Choose your path with eyes wide open, and do not get discouraged if the going gets rough and you cannot do it at all. Helping some young people traverse the mountain of modernity without falling and get through the swamp of youth culture without drowning is a great victory for the kingdom of God."[17]

I don't think the ancient, grimy couch is going to make its way into the sanctuary of the church anytime soon. However, I pray that those things the couch represents, and what good youth ministry represents, last for years to come.

REMODELING TIP

Two things are expedient to remember: The first is that we're not trying to create two churches in one. The New Testament presents a model of church that's cohesive, full of different kinds of folks—young and old, rich and poor, multiethnic, and multicultural (Titus 2:1-10). Amidst these differences, the New Testament church is tightly unified.

Youth ministry isn't a church of its own. While its methods may differ slightly due to its call to youth, it's still part of the church. Thus, ministering in ways that are radically different from the established majority, usually for the sake of difference, can result in division, even resulting in two separate churches under one roof. Division is harmful to the church.

Second, as youth ministers, we're not raising boys that can shave and girls that look like women. Instead, we, or rather God through us, are growing them to be the men and women God created them to be who will love Jesus and impact the world for His sake.

We don't want to perpetuate adolescence for decades. While creativity isn't bad, SpongeBob SquarePants shouldn't be teaching the youth group. That's not preparing them—and it's not preparing the church—for what Christ needs them to be. We should free them from feeling as if they need the latest gimmick. Instead, we want them to become responsible, helpful, contributing adults.

- **Jonathan Locklear,** Student Ministries Pastor, Woodhaven Free Will Baptist Church, Woodhaven, Michigan

---

Discussion Questions

1. What practices are used in churches today that were used only in youth ministry—but not "big church"—in the past?
2. How have you seen practices from youth ministry transition into the rest of the local church?
3. In what ways have youth ministries affected the local church positively or negatively?

4. What are the implications of youth ministry being a technology?
5. In what ways have you been deeply affected by your time in youth ministry?
6. What ways can your youth ministry positively affect the local church in the future?

Helpful Resources

Thomas Bergler, *The Juvenilization of American Christianity* (Grand Rapids, Mich.: Eerdmans, 2012).

"Forever Young," *Mortification of Spin Podcast*, May 27, 2015; http://www.alliancenet.org/mos/podcast/forever-young#.WNp5YjLMyCQ; accessed January 20, 2017; Internet.

Mark H. Senter, *When God Shows Up: A History of Protestant Youth Ministry in America* (Grand Rapids, Mich.: Baker Academic, 2010).

Christian Smith and Patricia Snell, *Souls in Transition: The Religious and Spiritual Lives of Emerging Adults* (New York: Oxford University Press, 2009).

"Youth Ministry and Youth Culture," *White Horse Inn Podcast*, June 22, 2014; https://www.white horseinn.org/2014/06/whi-1211-youth-ministry-youth-culture/; accessed January 17, 2017; Internet.

PART II

MAKING RENOVATIONS

CHAPTER 4

BEING MISSIONAL AS A TEENAGER

"Give students the message of God so they can spend their lives living out the mission of God."

- ALVIN REID[1]

I remember growing up watching reruns with my dad of the old *Mission: Impossible* television series. Agent Jim Phelps, played by actor Peter Graves, would receive a recording, giving him an incredible assignment, if he chose to accept it. Of course, he always did. Then, he would lead his team of IMF (Impossible Missions Force) agents to accomplish these impossible missions—hence the title.

Most of all, I remember the opening sequence in which a bomb wick burned as the theme music played, "Dun, dun, dah-dah, dun, dun, dah-dah, dun, dun." Every time my brother and I, as young boys, imagined ourselves as secret agents, we'd start to hum that theme song. It was the background noise to our epic adventures. Few make-believe villains were vanquished without either my brother or me providing that dramatic score.

Undoubtedly, these spec-op missions were all fiction.

Whether by an actor on a screen, or my siblings and me in the backyard, our missions were fully fabricated. No amount of sincerity, solid acting, or creativity could bring those missions to life. They were simply entertainment, an escape from the mundaneness of life.

As Christians, though, we *do* have a mission from God, the *missio Dei*. Of course, our message doesn't self-destruct in five seconds. Instead, it's directly tied to our mission: God's call on our lives to live according to His will, or to live missionally. God has given us a mission that radically transforms our purpose in this world. This mission from God is, at least in part, summed up in Matthew 28:18-20:

> And Jesus came and said to them, "All authority in heaven and on earth has been given to me. Go therefore and make disciples of all nations, baptizing them in the name of the Father and of the Son and of the Holy Spirit, teaching them to observe all that I have commanded you. And behold, I am with you always, to the end of the age."

This has often been called the Great Commission. In it, Jesus tells His disciples, which now include us, to make disciples and to teach them all that He has commanded.

When I think about the missional living that we envision for our students, my mind turns to Isaiah's call from God. In Isaiah 6, Isaiah, after hearing that King Uzziah had died, received a vision of God. He saw God in full majesty, His robe filling the entire temple and two, six-winged angels flying around Him, singing to one another, "Holy, holy, holy."

Seeing this incomprehensible sight, Isaiah was woefully aware of his own sin, stating it outright for all to hear. But God, instead of leaving Isaiah in his grief, sent a coal from the altar, the place of sacrifice, to cleanse Isaiah's sinfulness. God then asked, "Whom shall I send, and who will go for us?" Isaiah, having seen God's glory and his sins removed, responded: "Here I am! Send me."

This is the answer we want to hear from our students. We want them to understand God's greatness and His grace in forgiving our sins. We want them to live their lives radically for God's gospel mission in this world. This doesn't simply mean the obligatory, once-a-year, weeklong evangelistic program.

While those opportunities are beneficial, we want to do more than that. We want to cultivate a missional culture in our youth ministries. This means that everything they do, see, and partake in is shaped by God's heart for the world. We want our students, their lives, and our ministries to hold the banner for what Christ has done, is doing, and will do in this world. The question remains: How do we cultivate this disposition?

A GOSPEL MOTIVATION

As we seek to promote a missional culture among our students, we should ensure that we build it upon a proper foundation in the life of students. They must have a proper motivation: They must have a gospel motivation.

For students to live out God's mission in their lives, three things are necessary. First, they must continually think on the supremacy of Christ, not only in their own lives but also in the entire cosmos.

Second, they must understand the gospel in light of the full story of Scripture. We can easily detach the good news of Jesus Christ from the rest of the Bible. However, the entire Bible *is* the good news of Christ.

Third, students must understand how the gospel applies to every dimension of the Christian life. By combining these three components, students will begin to be motivated to live missionally in their lives today.

Comprehending the Supremacy of Christ

In his classic book *The Knowledge of the Holy*, A. W. Tozer famously penned these words: "What comes into our minds when we think about God is the most important thing about us."[2] Consider that: What we think about God changes our entire lives. If I think that God is nothing but wrathful, angry, and judging, that will affect the way I behave. Or if I think that God is nothing but gracious, caring, and loving, that too will affect me in the opposite way.

For this reason, we must have a biblical understanding of God. Do you want your students to see God in His glory, majesty, beauty, wonder, and preeminence? Turn to Paul's letter to the church at Colossae:

> He is the image of the invisible God, the firstborn of all creation. For by him all things were created, in heaven and on earth, visible and invisible, whether thrones or dominions or rulers or authorities—all things were created through him and for him. And

> he is before all things, and in him all things hold together. And he is the head of the body, the church. He is the beginning, the firstborn from the dead, that in everything he might be preeminent. For in him all the fullness of God was pleased to dwell, and through him to reconcile to himself all things, whether on earth or in heaven, making peace by the blood of his cross (1:15-19).

Paul didn't stop there. His understanding of Christ's supremacy was tied deeply to his ministry of the gospel: "And you, who once were alienated and hostile in mind, doing evil deeds, he has now reconciled in his body of flesh by his death, in order to present you holy and blameless and above reproach before him," Paul continued, "if indeed you continue in the faith, stable and steadfast, not shifting from the hope of the gospel that you heard, which has been proclaimed in all creation under heaven, and of which I, Paul, became a minister" (1:21-23).

Richard Ross perceptively writes, "Perhaps teenagers and adults have settled for sleepy, sentimental, scaled-down versions of the One who reigns supreme. Perhaps they seldom see Christ as Lord over creation, over history, over the church, and over all the ages to come."[3]

Too often our students settle for what Christian Smith calls "Moralistic Therapeutic Deism" (MTD).[4] In his seminal National Study of Youth and Religion, Smith found that the majority of teenagers' *de facto* faith in United States wasn't biblical Christianity but rather MTD. This worldview consists of five main tenets:

1. A God exists who created and orders the world and watches over human life on earth.
2. God wants people to be good, nice, and fair to each other, as taught in the Bible and by most world religions.
3. The central goal of life is to be happy and to feel good about one-self.
4. God does not need to be particularly involved in one's life except when he is needed to resolve a problem.
5. Good people go to heaven when they die.[5]

On the surface, this may sound like the truth of Scrip-ture, but it falls desperately short. MTD is intensely man-centered, almost explicitly stating that God exists solely for the purpose of man's happiness and comfort. God doesn't exist for us; we exist for Him and His glory. God isn't living out our mission; we're living out His mission.

For this reason, you should push your students to think about the glories of Christ. Push them to comprehend how awe-inspiring our God truly is. "The higher Jesus is lifted," Ross writes, "the greater the Father He reveals. A rising tide lifts all boats. A rising Christology lifts theology, discipleship, lordship, ecclesiology, and family ministry."[6] Of course, the only way to accomplish this is to point them to Scripture. Show them how God has revealed Himself to us in amazing ways. This leads us to ask whom the story of the Bible truly is about.

Telling the Story of Scripture

Is the story of Scripture primarily about God or me? The answer to that question is vital. If, every time that I open my

Bible, I simply ask about myself and not about God, then I'll walk away with answers to questions about me and not about God or anything else.

On the other hand, if I ask questions about God, then I come away with answers about who God is and what He's like and what He's doing in the world. The answers to these questions provide a foundation for answering questions about my life and the world. C. S. Lewis memorably quipped, "Aim at Heaven and you will get Earth 'thrown in': aim at Earth and you will get neither."[7]

Don't take my word for it. The Bible offers an explicit answer to the question of whom the Bible is ultimately about. Luke 24:25-27 details the story of Jesus walking with two disciples on the road to Emmaus. After the two disciples explain what had just happened in Jerusalem, Jesus said to them, "'O foolish ones, and slow of heart to believe all that the prophets have spoken! Was it not necessary that the Christ should suffer these things and enter into his glory?' And beginning with Moses and all the Prophets, he interpreted to them in all the Scriptures the things concerning himself" (24:25b-27).

Later, speaking to His disciples, Jesus affirmed this same point:

> Then he said to them, "These are my words that I spoke to you while I was still with you, that everything written about me in the Law of Moses and the Prophets and the Psalms must be fulfilled." Then he opened their minds to understand the Scriptures, and said to them, "Thus it is written, that the Christ

> should suffer and on the third day rise from the dead, and that repentance and forgiveness of sins should be proclaimed in his name to all nations, beginning from Jerusalem. You are witnesses of these things (24:44-48).

For students to live out God's mission for their lives fully, they need a have a story to tell. That story is the story of Scripture. From beginning to end, it attests to the mighty and wonderful acts of God. In both the individual stories and the overall story, the Bible proclaims a message that students can share. As Alvin Reid notes, "Missional means showing unbelievers the gospel from the perspective of their worldview, moving them to see a biblical idea."[8]

For students to live out and share the gospel, they must be immersed in the truth of God's Word. Reid states further, "The mission of God is central to all of Scripture, all of creation, all of history, and therefore, all of life. . . . Give students the message of God so they can spend their lives living out the mission of God."[9] This is our charge as youth ministers.

In Ezekiel 37, God commanded the prophet to speak to a valley of dry bones. Very literally, He asked him to preach to a pile of dead bodies. Ezekiel was faithful, doing what the LORD commanded. But as he did so, he saw the transformation that God's Word had on those bones. Flesh began to come upon them, and life entered into them.

In many ways, Ezekiel 37 is a parable for our own preaching and teaching. As we preach and teach to the spiritually dead and lifeless, we have the privilege of watching

God's Word transform students and bring life—and life more abundantly. As youth workers, we have the most powerful force in the cosmos, the Word of God. Let's put that Word into the hands of teenagers so that they may radically change the world.

Alan Stewart writes, "People will be motivated to evangelize when they realize it is the whole thrust of the Bible."[10] We want students to emulate the heart of God, and the only way for them to discover that on their own is by reading and hearing His Word. Once students begin to see the supremacy of God not only in their own lives but also in Scripture, they'll begin to see the wide reach of the gospel.

The Gospel for Life

To encourage missional living in our students, we must demonstrate to them the reach of the gospel. The gospel isn't simply the entrance door into the Christian life; it's the entirety of the Christian life. Too often we talk about the gospel only as a way into becoming a Christian instead of explaining how it's connected to every area of the believer's life. Unfortunately, in both youth ministry and the larger ministry of the church, we've relegated the gospel to a canned evangelistic presentation. That's a poor, pitiful view of God's good news.

Rather, the gospel speaks to every sphere of existence. As youth ministry expert David Hertweck states, "The message of the Gospel is not something that is solely necessary at the beginning of a teenager's faith journey; it is their faithful companion every step of the way. We never graduate from the truth of the Gospel, rather we cling to it and allow it to bring about more and more change in our lives."[11] Indeed, the gospel gives us a new understanding of the world.

God's action within reality reorients all of life. In the Christian worldview, the gospel is the epicenter of a world completely turned upside-down. Because Christ has changed our hearts, our lives, and our understanding of the world, nothing about us is the same. Thus, we must show and tell our students how the gospel affects all of life. We must show, in Christ's gospel, a new and better understanding of, for example, marriage (Ephesians 5:22-33), work (2 Thessalonians 3:6-12), ministry (2 Corinthians 5:20), and children (Mark 10:13-16). Recognizing that the gospel is for all of life will lead us to sharing fully the *missio Dei* with our students.

WORK IN THE *MISSIO DEI*

If we limit gospel content only to evangelism, then we've failed to understand fully the mission of God. As one author said, we should "gospelize everything."[12] That's not to say that we make loose connections and poor analogies to our evangelistic call. It doesn't mean that we use the gospel as a reduced adjective.

Instead, we should show students how the gospel affects every aspect of our youth ministry and ultimately our lives. How, for example, can students see the gospel in the way that we oversee lock-ins, conduct Bible lessons, or spend time with one another over a meal? Because Christ has sent His Spirit to indwell and empower those who trust in Him, we're changed.

When our students are in union with Christ, that union changes everything. Greg Stier, founder and president of Dare 2 Share ministries, says, "At the core of the heart of Jesus is a desperate search-and-rescue mission for the lost."[13] If that's the heart of Jesus, then it ought also to be the heart of youth ministries.

Stephen Ingram states, "It is so easy to assume that our job is limited to being the ones who facilitate and lead ministries. But youth ministry comes full circle only when we empower our students to become agents of mission, not just recipients, to lead us in ministry, to inspire us to action and service."[14] If your students are living missionally, then they'll work to transform the culture around them; they'll aim to bring gospel light and redemption to a sin-distorted world.

We see this in the Great Commission. It's imperative is not "go" but rather "make disciples." The word translated "go," Reid rightly notes, should be understood as a continuous action, meaning that it's better translated "as you go" (Matthew 28:19-20).[15]

For that reason, living missionally is not so much about going to faraway countries, though it may include that. It's more about living on mission wherever God has placed you. As you go through life, in whatever spheres of influence God has given you, you're seeking to bring redemption and transformation via the gospel to a sinful world. As F. Leroy Forlines said, "We are supposed to be transforming the secular culture rather than to be transformed by it."[16]

This means your students are not only sharing the

gospel message, but they're practicing it as well. Their minds and actions are not being conformed to this world but rather are being transformed by Christ (Romans 12:1-2). They're seeking to proclaim the good news of Jesus Christ to those who haven't heard it, as well as seeking to apply the gospel in their homes, schools, jobs, and relationships. They're combining orthodoxy (right teaching) with orthopraxy (right living).

They're telling people the only truth that can change their eternity by proclaiming the gospel. At the same time, they're feeding the hungry, helping the downcast, and caring for the marginalized. Your students should have ample opportunities to go and tell the gospel through evangelistic opportunities. Simultaneously, they should find opportunities to help at the nearby crisis pregnancy center, soup kitchens, and non-profit educational centers. This is the *missio Dei* in the world.[17] We're called to emulate God's redemptive work in the world.

God has called our students to a more-than-average, *status quo* life. He's called us to share a life-giving message to the world around us (Matthew 24:14; Psalm 96:3; Romans 1:16). We should be bold in this proclamation, remembering that it's the world's only hope.

Included in this message is the goal to transform this world through our actions (Isaiah 65; Amos 5:15, 24; Romans 5:12-21; 8:19-22; 12:1-2). We accomplish this by applying God's truth to every situation we're given. Ultimately, it's up to us as youth workers to motivate our students to this missional living by grounding them in the truth of the gospel.

REMODELING TIP

One of the greatest joys in ministry is to hear a student talk about his or her conversation pertaining to the gospel. I've seen numerous students who've had the "Aha!" moment that every youth pastor looks for. It's in that moment that the gospel penetrates their hearts to the point that they want to share it with others.

The most impactful moment I've seen was when I shared the following with my students: Your faith can be more far-reaching than you can imagine if you'd just live out and share the gospel before those in your schools. In our suburban ministry setting, we're very spread out. We have just over thirty students in more than twenty schools with the potential to reach more than thirty thousand students in their different schools.

For the missions trips we take each summer, students receive more than six months of training about myriad topics to help them grow in their faith and to challenge them to live in light of this faith before others. By the time we reach our missions destination, students have been challenged to dig deep into the Bible and to share the gospel with friends. The day I received a text from a student in a summer program explaining that she'd just led a friend to Christ was a day that I won't soon forget.

All in all, when a student recognizes that the gospel has the power to change lives (Romans 1:16), and when they unleash that power, ministry becomes the most fun and rewarding job you could ever have.

- **Ryan Akers,** Pastor to Students, Calvary Fellowship Free Will Baptist Church, Fenton, Missouri

Discussion Questions

1. What is the *misiso Dei*?
2. In what ways can students live missionally in their lives today?
3. In what ways can the youth worker motivate his or her students in the gospel?
4. How does the gospel apply to every area of our lives?

5. How does the supremacy of God affect our understanding of the gospel and Great Commission?
6. We might interpret the beginning of the Great Commission as "as you go." How does that change our understanding of evangelism?
7. In what ways does telling the whole story of Scripture equip our students to be more missional?

Helpful Resources

Greg Gilbert, *What is the Gospel?* (Wheaton, Ill.: Crossway, 2010).

John Owen, *The Glory of Christ*, Puritan Paperback (Carlisle, Penn.: The Banner of Truth Trust, 1994).

Alvin Reid, *As You Go: Creating a Missional Culture of Gospel-Centered Students* (Colorado Springs: THINK, 2013).

Richard Ross, *Student Ministry and the Supremacy of Christ* (Bloomington, Ind.: Cross, 2009).

Alan Stewart, ed., *No Guts, No Glory: How to Build a Youth Ministry That Lasts* (Kingsford, NSW, Australia: Matthias Media, 2000).

Christopher Wright, *The Mission of God's People: A Biblical Theology of the Church's Mission* (Grand Rapids, Mich.: Zondervan, 2010).

CHAPTER 5

MEANS OF GRACE AND METHODOLOGY

"America's youth not only need *a ministry that seeks to communicate God's grace through the teaching of the Word, administration of the [ordinances], a life of prayer, gospel-motivated ministry, and grace-centered community—they actually* want *such a ministry."*

- BRIAN COSBY[I]

I remember my wedding day vividly. Of all the important events of my life, my wedding day stands above them all (excepting my conversion). Full of nerves and excitement, I was ready to step out of the side room of the sanctuary and see my future wife. In the moments before, I had given the wedding ring to my brother. We heard the musical cue, and we walked out in front of the congregation. I stood, trying to maintain some semblance of control as I waited—eagerly, emotionally, excitedly—to see my bride.

The grandparents were seated, then the parents. Our bridal party walked in with smiles on their faces, looking at me as if they'd heard some good news before I did. Then the moment I was waiting for: my wife and my father-in-law turned the corner. The lump in my throat seemed to come out of nowhere. It must have been dusty in there, because my eyes began to water. Although this may sound cliché, it was as if time itself had stopped. My eyes were fixed on my wife.

As I took her hand and led her up to the platform, we began the ceremony that would mark the beginning of the rest of our lives together. There were numerous meaningful things we did during that ceremony. We exchanged rings, stated vows, and committed ourselves to one another.

We also participated in a practice that you don't often see at weddings: We washed one another's feet. Feetwashing is a distinctive practice of my own denomination,practiced in response of Christ's command in John 13:12-14: "When he had washed their feet and put on his outer garments and resumed his place, he said to them, 'Do you understand what I have done to you? You call me Teacher and Lord, and you are right, for so I am. If I then, your Lord and Teacher, have washed your feet, you also ought to wash one another's feet.'"[2]

Whether you agree that this should be a church ordinance is beside the point. In that moment of our wedding, my wife and I were displaying something to each other and to all the witnesses gathered. We were demonstrating that we're committed to humbling ourselves in order to serve the other person. In a very real sense, we were demonstrating that we're committed to living out Ephesians 5:22-33 in our marriage. We wanted the gospel to be on display in the wedding ceremony itself.

Why is my wedding day relevant to youth ministry? The practices we perpetuate in our youth ministries teach and form our students in their Christian walk. What we teach as important and demonstrate as vital shapes our students in powerful ways. We should ensure that we're thinking holistically and critically about the different methods and practices that we use in our ministry to students.

We might ask questions like: What does this practice teach about sanctification? How are my students being taught to grow in godliness? Can my students see from the Word how they are to grow in godliness? Are my methods contradicting my theology? Does my ministry demonstrate my trust in Scripture? How are my methods being influenced by the surrounding culture?

THE NEED FOR CHANGE

With these questions in mind, take a snapshot of current youth ministry methodology. Undoubtedly a tension emerges between what young people want and what they need. That tension often lies at the heart of youth ministry.[3] Due to our consumer-driven culture, the desires of youth are often fed through entertainment. As we've already considered, this isn't a recent development—the blood has been in the water for some time.

During the 1940s, the Youth for Christ movement pioneered entertainment-driven youth ministry. They tried to Christianize the youth entertainment of their day with a set list of vaudeville-style gimmicks: a performing "gospel horse," a faux Frank Sinatra, and a fun-focused message.

Thomas Bergler explains, "For the leaders of the Youth for Christ, Christianity was increasingly becoming a product to be sold to customers via entertaining promises of personal fulfillment—with an added benefit of saving the world."[4]

It's easy for us to identify these approaches as gimmicks, being removed by several decades. However, hindsight is always twenty-twenty. It's more difficult to identify such forms as gimmicky when we're immersed in them; and today, many youth ministries are immersed in an updated version of the same thing.

The numbers show that we're in a crisis mode. Study after study, from LifeWay to TIME magazine, states that the church is losing youth in droves. This can easily put us in panic mode. It causes us to double-down on our current youth ministry practices. With no other options and with numbers staring us in the face, we're given to reinforce what we've always done. However, it's become increasingly clear that the silver bullet of youth ministry isn't found in these past approaches.

Fast-forward to today and many are lamenting the state of an entertainment-driven youth ministry. Any minister trying to chase a higher shock-factor will quickly realize that the law of diminished returns applies to youth ministry.[5] Each time we do something bigger and better, we're expected to top it with the next activity. Entertainment-driven models attract by promising short-term, numeric results, while claiming to "reach kids for Christ."

However, these same ministries often forget the second half of the Great Commission: teaching them all that Christ has commanded. With such an emphasis on engaging students and grabbing their attention, we've often failed to lead them into deeper discipleship. This forces us to ask the question: How do we know that we're reaching students if we're not seeing them mature in Christ?

To steal a phrase from Cosby, we can begin reform in our youth ministries by "giving up the gimmicks."[6] Founder of Young Life Jim Rayburn allegedly said, "It's a sin to bore a kid."[7] While Rayburn was most likely advocating for entertainment, Cosby notes, "[Youth] are bored because they are living from one pleasure high to the next. They're not encouraged to live out, for example, the content and method of ministry service." He continues, "America's youth not only *need* a ministry that seeks to communicate God's grace through the teaching of the Word, administration of the [ordinances], a life of prayer, gospel-motivated ministry, and grace-centered community—they actually *want* such a ministry."[8]

Giving students what they need is better than giving them what they want. A holistic means of grace ministry accomplishes both. The means of grace include the Word, ordinances, prayer, service (ministry), church discipleship, the spiritual disciplines, and all other practices God has ordained in the Scripture.[9]

These are the very means by which God reveals His steadfast, committed love and grace to those who put their faith in Him. That's not to say that these practices work *ex opere operato* ("by the work performed"), or magically produce results.[10] Rather, God works through these means because He has ordained them for the building of the church.

These are the means that Scripture prescribes, not only

for teenagers but for all Christians, to grow in godliness. They're not *common* grace means but *special* grace means; they're grace made effectual in believers' lives via God's redemptive grace.[11] As the Christian is made new by Christ, His Spirit participates in each of these means of grace. As this occurs, the Christian will begin to love God's Word more, love his or her neighbor more, and hunger for God more.

An unashamed commitment to the sufficiency of Scripture undergirds these means of grace in the life of our ministry. All of the means of grace are established in the Bible and practiced in the early church. Acts 2:42, for example, states, "And they *devoted* themselves to the apostles' *teaching* and the *fellowship*, to the *breaking of bread* and the *prayers*."[12] We too should allow the means of grace to become our "strategy" for ministry. As we do this, we'll begin to see their sufficiency and ultimately the sufficiency of Christ and His Word.

CONNECTING MEANS AND METHODOLOGY

One large question still remains: How do these means of grace translate into methods? Our goal is that these means transform our students into the image of Christ. Thus, we need to implement them into the life of our ministries and watch God work through them. Rather than allowing videos, games, or events to become the focal point of youth ministry, let God's means of grace shape your practices. This makes the temporal elements of our ministry secondary. Biblical content and methods of ministry cannot be divorced.[13]

The crux of this paradigm shift is a desire to see Christian students living their lives in a countercultural way. Foundationally, this means that they must understand their spirituality, the means by which they grow in godliness, in a different way than the world. Fred Edie asks, "Do we as Christians believe any longer that our spiritual convictions manifest themselves in distinctive or even countercultural ways of living in the world?"[14]

These means of grace give us exactly that—a different pattern of life. We're teaching our students to live counterculturally and to practice habits that make them stand out in the world. Let's look at how some of these might look in a given youth ministry.

Biblical Proclamation: ". . . to the apostles teaching . . ."

First, and primary, is biblical proclamation (covered more thoroughly in chapter nine). This comes in a variety of different forms. Even though you're ministering primarily to youth, every youth pastor is still a pastor. And every pastor's primary responsibility is to "preach the Word" (2 Timothy 4:2).

The youth pastor should look for specific and particular times in which he can preach to his flock of students. This doesn't mean that youth pastors should have their own, separate worship service each week. However, your students should be getting, along with the sermon from the senior pastor, a consistent and robust diet of expositional preaching and teaching from their youth pastor.

Additionally, if a youth pastor is seeking to fulfill this command, all of their lessons should be expositional. That doesn't mean that each lesson must be a verse-by-verse journey through a given passage (though that's not a bad idea). Instead, your teaching should explain and unpack God's Word (2 Timothy 2:15). Remember this: How you teach your students is as important as what you teach your students. How you teach is teaching your students how to study the Bible.

Of course, our teaching and preaching of the Bible shouldn't simply lead to a headful of Bible facts. We teach and preach Scripture because we want it to transform our students in every dimension of their lives. We proclaim biblical truth to cause our students to worship more. As one author writes, "If the fundamental gift and call to Christ's Body in the world is the love of God and the love of neighbor, then worship will ever be the primary and principal practice of Christian life."[15]

Fellowship: ". . . and the fellowship . . ."

Second, we can help our students grow in godliness by helping them fellowship with other believers. Notice that I didn't say fellowship with other teenagers. It's well and good for students to spend time with other Christians their age, but we should also help them strive for spiritual maturity by spending time with Christians that are older and younger than they are.

Older saints can show younger students what living out the faith looks like for decade after decade. At the same time, as students spend time with those younger than them, they'll have the opportunity to mentor those less mature in the faith.

Our fellowship should break cultural categories. We need to give our students opportunities to listen, watch, and interact with those that look nothing like them. Only by practicing fellowship like this can we start to demonstrate for our youth what a countercultural, covenant community looks like (we'll discuss this further in chapter seven).

Of course, fellowship is distinct from socializing. Socializing means that we're spending time with other people, often characterized by sharing life together. Fellowship is all about the Christian life. You know that you're spending time in fellowship when you focus on the spiritual dimensions of life, discussing and living out what walking with Christ means.

Prayer: ". . . and the prayers . . ."

Third, we must lead our students in prayer. Prayer is not the Christian's magic formula to a stress-free life. It's not some sort of divine reset button when life is hard. We can pray earnestly, and yet God may choose to keep us in our present circumstances, whatever the difficulty.

Prayer is less about changing God's mind and more about changing ours.[16] Prayer changes our will rather than changes God's. Prayer gives us an opportunity to commune with our Creator, the God of the universe. That cannot leave us unchanged. John Bunyan, the famous Puritan, defined prayer this way: "Prayer is a sincere, sensible, affectionate pouring out of the heart or soul to God, through Christ, in the strength and assistance of the Holy Spirit, for such things as God has promised, or according to his Word, for the good of the church, with submission in faith to the will of God."[17]

Scripture must shape our prayers as we lead students in this practice. This characteristic is true of all of the means of grace. We must think, then, about the types of prayers we see in Scripture. When leading my students, I try to help them put their prayers into three specific categories: (1) repentance, (2) rejoicing, and (3) requests. These categories help our students from treating God like a spiritual butler, inquiring with a long list of demands.

Instead, they're repenting of their lack of holiness (Psalm 51). They're rejoicing in God's goodness and beauty (Habakkuk 3). They're also petitioning God for certain things in their lives (Psalm 4; 7). You may also encourage your students to pray in different contexts. Give them opportunities to pray corporately, leading other students in prayer. Allow them to pray individually, speaking to God with personal requests. Give them prayer partners so that they know someone is committed to praying for them and so that they can pray for someone.

Service: "And they devoted themselves . . ."

Fourth, we should give our students opportunities to serve in the church and community. Your students will most likely find themselves on either end of a long spectrum concerning service. Either they won't want to help anyone ever, or they'll want to do grand things for God. While the latter is certainly preferred, service occurs most often in everyday opportunities.

Donald Whitney, Professor of Biblical Spirituality at the Southern Baptist Theological Seminary, writes, "Although Christ's summons to service is the most spiritually grand and noble way to live a life, it is typically as pedestrian as washing someone's feet."[18] This is the precise example that Christ gave to us (John 13:12-14). Service is primarily about humbling yourself so that you might be able to help others. Thus, two things are required: (1) a humble spirit and (2) a desire to serve. Certainly, these two elements walk hand in hand.

What might this look like in your youth ministry? Plenty of opportunities are available in your immediate church for service. There are often shut-ins that would be delighted to spend some time with young people. Your church can rake leaves in the community or host a mother's day out. On a bigger scale, you can get your students to volunteer at the local homeless mission or the food pantry. This connects our words with our actions (Matthew 25:31-46). Not only are we teaching about the sanctity of human life, but we're also demonstrating it through our acts of service.

Ordinances: ". . . to the breaking of bread . . . "

Finally, we should lead our students in the ordinances. My denomination, Free Will Baptists, include the following practices as ordinances of the church: (1) baptism, (2) the Lord's Supper, and (3) the washing of the saints' feet. J. Matthew Pinson defines an ordinance as "a practice that God ordained for literal perpetuation by the New Covenant People of God."[19] Simply, an ordinance is a practice that the Bible prescribes for the continual practice of believers everywhere.

Why should we include the ordinances in the means of grace, especially for youth ministry? Isn't that something for "big church"? Well, yes and no. Each of these ordinances should be practiced within the fully gathered local church. Thus, we should practice them with our students.

By partaking in these ordinances, they show their inclusion in the body of Christ. When students are baptized, they're not only testifying of their new life to their friends but also to the entire gathered body of believers. When students partake in the Lord's Supper and the washing of the saints' feet, they're learning that they're part of something much bigger than themselves, the bride of Christ that stretches through space and time.

These ordinances also serve as a visualization of the gospel for our students. Baptism shows how we're buried in death with Christ and raised anew in His resurrection. The Lord's Supper reminds us that Christ's body was crucified and His blood shed in order for our sins to be forgiven, which we can experience if we're in union with Him. The washing of the saints' feet demonstrates the grand humility of our Lord, not only as He washed His disciples' feet but also in signifying His incarnation.

The ordinances of the church are constant visual gospel reminders for our students. For that reason, practice them with your students often and consistently.

REMODELING TIP

Ten years of youth ministry have changed my view of what constitutes success. I used to judge success by the volume of the music and the enthusiasm for "gross-out" games. Over time, I've learned that you often don't see the fruit of a youth ministry until years afterward. Are the students from your youth group still serving, loving, and growing in their local church years later? That's youth ministry fruit.

If we're going to help the church rebound from a generation of failed youth ministry, we need the vision cast in this chapter. This won't be easy, or even popular, because its strategies aren't what spring to most minds when you think about youth ministry; but it will be fruitful.

We often think that we can't compete with the world's attractions—with their "methodology" and their "means of grace," if you will. But truthfully the world can't compete with ours either. We have God to offer our teens: God in Word and ordinance, God in deed and love. Do you believe this, brother youth pastor? Our challenge is to put away the parodies and to embrace the power of God for the sake of our teenagers.

Let's not dumb down our Bible teaching, but rather let's stretch our students, bathing them in the heart-shaping, life-giving glory of God. Let's not simply plan activities, but rather let's create meaningful opportunities for our teenagers to learn from and serve seasoned saints. Let's not simply plan youth services, but rather let's involve them in greeting, ushering, and nursery working regularly.

Recover a belief in the beauty and necessity of prayer and the ordinances and take your students on the journey with you. Then, by God's grace, as we use His methods, youth ministry will, slowly but surely, produce the fruit in keeping with repentance.

- **Ed Goode,** Associate Pastor, First Church - a Free Will Baptist Fellowship, Richmond, Virginia

---

FIRST THINGS

If Scripture is made central, then preaching, teaching, and memorizing it will become a priority. As we saturate our youth ministry in individual and corporate prayer, a beautiful picture of our dialogue with God will be painted. While we follow the biblical models for discipleship, we'll see the community of our youth group take biblical rather than pragmatic form.

Our focus on service will cultivate cultural awareness and biblical application. And as we serve with our students, they'll see our life lived out in light of the gospel. As we observe biblical ordinances, we'll note the beautiful symbolism of Christ's servanthood, death, and resurrection. These means of grace are formative in the minds of young people.

We must keep first things first. It's not that we don't do other things in our youth ministry. However, we want to make sure that these means of grace, the ways in which God has told us to grow His church, are front and center in our youth ministries. If we allow these elements to become our means, then we'll display the sufficiency of Christ in our ministry. If the maxim of "what you win them with is what you win them to" is true, then Christ must occupy the center of our ministry and methods.

Discussion Questions

1. What are the means of grace?
2. What are some examples of how the means of grace form our students' lives?
3. In what ways do baptism and other ritual ordinances demonstrate the gospel?
4. Where do we find the means of grace in Scripture?
5. What is the difference between socializing and fellowship?
6. What are practical ways to implement the means of grace in youth ministry?

Helpful Resources

John Bunyan, *Prayer,* Puritan Paperbacks (Carlisle, Penn.: The Banner of Truth Trust, 2012).

Brian H. Cosby, *Giving Up Gimmicks: Reclaiming Youth Ministry from an Entertainment Culture* (Phillipsburg, N.J.: P&R, 2012).

Mark Howard, "Fun and Substance in Youth Ministry," *Rooted Ministry,* October 20, 2013; https://www.rootedministry.com/blog/fun-and-substance-in-youth-ministry/; accessed January 12, 2017. Internet.

J. Matthew Pinson, *The Washing of the Saints' Feet* (Nashville: Randall House, 2006).

Donald S. Whitney, *Spiritual Disciplines for the Christian Life* (Colorado Springs: NavPress, 1991).

CHAPTER 6

RETHINKING APOLOGETICS FOR STUDENTS

"No one can become a Christian unless he understands what Christianity is saying."

- FRANCIS SCHAEFFER[I]

I've often said that modern youth ministry puts the correct emphasis in two places: evangelism and apologetics. While other elements of youth ministry are debatable, there's hardly a youth group I know that doesn't consistently emphasize these areas—and rightly so. In many ways, evangelism and apologetics represent the foundational dimension of a student's faith. How a student articulates his or her faith, while also defending that faith, is a helpful barometer to discern the student's commitment to and maturity in the faith.

Apologetics refers to the practice of defending the faith. Descending from the Greek word *apologia,* it literally means "defense." The word has the connotation of a courtroom in which someone gives reasoned arguments to convince the skeptic. For that reason, a Christian apologist (someone who does apologetics) defends, communicates, and convinces others of the truth of Christianity. Apologetics can also be used to encourage other believers in the faith, assuring them of the truth in which they've believed.

Nevertheless, I've been surprised in my teaching of future youth ministers. If you had asked me before I began teaching youth and family ministry what the number one question I might hear the most, I would have struggled to answer. I may have speculated that students would inquire about curriculum (which they have), activities, or even the magic equation of ordering the right amount of pizza (a professional secret). Still, the one question I hear from aspiring youth ministers more than any other, interestingly enough, is about apologetics.

Students consistently ask me if I know of any apologetic resources that focus more heavily on worldview issues, or what Leroy Forlines calls the "inescapable questions of life." He writes,

> Every human being has what I call the inescapable questions of life. Is there a God? If so, how can I know him? How can I know what is right and wrong? Is there life after death? If so, how can I get ready for it? A person may give the wrong answers, but he cannot keep from asking the right questions. Why does every person have these questions? I believe it is because God has designed us so that as we develop into thinking individuals these questions will naturally arise within us. We are not a blank tablet upon which we can choose what we want to be written and be happy with any choice we might make. Our needs have been designed in us by God. They are innate. As

> we develop, it is inevitable that these questions will arise within us.[2]

Most of these students have access to plenty of resources concerning archeology, history, science, and other topics to defend their faith. Rather, they're seeking an apologetical method that deals more centrally with the various presuppositions found in their world.

We could sit back and critique the current state of youth ministry; I've done very thing. However, I don't believe we should completely reorient how we teach apologetics in youth ministry. Instead, we should make a slight course correction and focus on what can make it better.

THE RIGHT DIRECTION

One of the main aims of apologetics in youth ministry is to help teenagers develop confidence in their faith and articulate a proper defense of it. The better teenagers can defend it, the more likely they will take possession of it, so the logic goes. Hardly anyone can disagree with this. Teaching apologetics is one of the best ways to instruct a student in acknowledging the truths of Christianity. For that reason, apologetics has become both prevalent and popular among Christian youth groups.

Amidst this healthy development, youth pastors must understand the globalized, media-saturated culture in which we live. We're not fighting competing worldviews simply on Sundays and Wednesdays. Turning on their televisions, looking at their cell phones, or glancing at their computers and tablets, youth are inundated with a variety of messages. These messages are often more implicit than explicit and more formative than informative. What's more, many of these messages, unsurprisingly, conflict with biblical Christianity.

For example, in an article for *The Atlantic*, Larry Taunton makes some striking claims about young atheists. Taunton and his team interviewed many young atheists to find some common denominators that led to their religious decisions. While one would expect these students to cite at least one of the new atheists,[3] Taunton and his team instead "heard vague references to videos they had watched on YouTube or website forums."[4]

While youth pastors are diligent to teach their students solid proofs for the legitimacy of Christianity, the world is drawing cultural maps for students to follow day by day. Even on social media, students are getting answers to their inescapable questions. The media with which they interact daily is shaping the way they view the world.

A SLIGHT CORRECTION

You might ask: "What should we change in apologetics for youth ministry?" Walt Mueller alludes to the answer:

> Adolescence is a crossroads. It is a time marked by overwhelming change, numerous questions and a search for answers. Not sure which direction to take, the emerging generations are presented with confusing messages and options. Usually the signposts they

> choose to follow are the most attractive, loud, and convincing in response to their unspoken teenage cry of "Show me the way." The choice is made easier when they see their peers moving en masse in one direction. The automatic assumption is, "That must be the way."[5]

Youth are looking for more than just answers. They're looking for a worldview. This is where we need to make an adjustment. This is where we need to think a little deeper about apologetics.

Broadly speaking, evidentialism and presuppositionalism are the two main schools of apologetics.[6] The titles are telling. The former tends to focus primarily with archeological, historical, and scientific proofs, or logical proofs for the existence of God, in order to substantiate a case for Christianity. The latter deals primarily with people and their worldview presuppositions.

Evidentialism

Paul Cowan explains evidentialism by saying, "Evidentialism as an apologetic method can be characterized as the 'one-step' approach. . . . [I]t tends to focus chiefly on the legitimacy of accumulating various historical and other inductive arguments for the truth of Christianity."[7] An evidential apologist will focus heavily on evidences to prove his or her case.

In many ways, this has proven helpful, not only for convincing the skeptic but also in affirming the faith of believers. At the same time, I'm concerned that evidential approaches don't deal adequately with how sin affects the human mind. The evidentialist presupposes (pun intended) that both believers and non-believers approach evidence on neutral grounds with objective perspectives.[8] However, reality attests that this is never the case. Christians and non-Christians think differently. For that reason, our apologetics should reflect that distinction.

Presuppostionalism

Concerning presuppositionalism, Cowan writes, "Due to the noetic effects of sin, presuppositionalists usually hold that there is not enough common ground between believers and unbelievers. . . . The apologist must simply presuppose the truth of Christianity as the proper starting point in apologetics. . . . Presuppositionalists . . . argue that all meaning and thought—indeed, every fact—logically presupposes the God of the Scriptures."[9]

I believe we should show unbelievers how God's truth revealed through Scripture answers all of life's questions in every sphere of life. We must show them that all of reality makes sense through a gospel worldview. John Frame explains, "[We] should present the biblical God, not merely as the conclusion to an argument, but as the one who makes argument possible."[10]

Francis Schaeffer advocated a similar approach, explaining that we have to "take the roof off" of inconsistent worldviews.[11] This means showing people how their lifestyles and choices are often inconsistent with the worldviews they espouse and how their worldviews are often inconsistent with reality.

A biblical worldview, on the other hand, offers a cohesive, consistent worldview for life. For example, we can explain how only Christianity gives a complete answer to the suffering we find in the world. We can demonstrate how biblical sexuality is better for human flourishing. We can show how Christian thinking combines all areas of knowledge.[12]

MAKING THE ADJUSTMENT

Our apologetics is where youth workers and ministers need to make an adjustment. In my experience, the majority of apologetical resources, as well as the teaching on the subject, have emphasized an evidential approach. While we shouldn't disregard evidences, which are often helpful, I believe that the millennial generation of students, living in the throes of postmodernism, requires a more presuppositional approach.

For example, imagine you're teaching the story of Noah. Undoubtedly, you might give your students archeological proof for the flood; at the same time, you might also challenge them to wrestle with God's judgment upon humanity. While the former deals with evidences, the latter concerns worldview presuppositions.

Take another example in the claims of Jesus Christ. We might give our students historical evidence concerning Jesus' historicity; but we might also help them to understand the exclusivity of Christ and the presuppositions entailed therein.

The impetus for my concern about overemphasizing evidences within youth ministry is this: Too much evidential apologetics may result for students simply in talking points about their faith. However, when students understand the presuppositions contained in different worldviews, they emerge with a more holistic understanding of their own faith and the world around them. In fact, presuppositions orient them better in their use of evidences.[13] So, while evidential apologetics may teach our students *what* to think, presuppositional apologetics will lead them in *how* to think.

To echo Mueller, these students find themselves at a crossroads trying to understand the world. As Schaeffer argues, the real question in apologetics is whether God's communication to us explains what we already know to be true.[14] Does God's special revelation to us fill in our understanding of the world?

REMODELING TIP

Our culture is masterfully, some may say deceitfully, conditioning the rising generations to dissociate with objective truth and embrace a more "tolerant" truth: relativism. Whether we realize it, this philosophy is rapidly growing in acceptance. However, this interpretation of reality does not truthfully interpret actual reality. If all things are true, then nothing is true.

Challenges like relativism are exactly why the inclusion of solid apologetics is vital for every student ministry. Though we're the most informed generations in human history (thank you, Google), the rising generations are also on pace to become the most skeptical generations in human history.

The church's ministry to these students must embrace the doubts and the hard questions that will come its way; too much is at stake not to do so. Developing a proper understanding of the Christian worldview is a strong apologetic against doubt. After all, apologetics helps fill the potholes on the road to salvation.

Students today long for authenticity. The Christian faith is the most authentic thing we student pastors could ever champion before them.

We must instill within our students a hunger for truth. If students hunger for truth, their appetite will eventually lead them to the Creator.

Why? Because truth isn't something that mankind has constructed; it's not something that we have constructed on a whim. Truth is the standard that the Creator of the universe has established. When our students develop a hunger to be truth seekers, they will inevitably become Truth ambassadors.

- **Aaron Pontious,** Student Pastor, The Donelson Fellowship, Nashville, Tennessee

---

APOLOGETICS IS NOT EVANGELISM

Apologetics is important. However, we must remember that it's not evangelism. Louis Markos writes, "Many today confuse apologetics with another branch of Christianity with which it bears much in common—evangelism; but the two are quite different in their focus and approach. . . . Whereas the evangelist is first and foremost a preacher, the apologist is essentially a teacher."[15]

I agree with Markos's observation, but I believe that the difference between evangelism and apologetics is more than that between preaching and teaching. The dividing line may be between the presentation of truth and the defense of that truth. We can explain and defend propositional truths all day long (apologetics), but unless we urgently plead with individuals to put their faith in *the truth* (evangelism), we haven't completed our call.

Schaeffer refers to apologetics as "pre-evangelism."[16] He explains that a person must have a right understanding of truth before he or she becomes a Christian.[17] Logically, believing comes before belonging. We must first hear and understand the Word of Christ before putting our faith in it (Romans 10:17). This means that a proper understanding of Christian truth is necessary to lead us into the body of Christ. Such thinking pushes back against certain modern understandings of youth ministry and church.

Many of those associated with the emergent church movement would baulk at this claim. In *Youth Ministry in a Post-Christian World*, Brock Morgan argues that we should reverse this order and tell students: "You can belong before you believe."[18] While I certainly empathize with Morgan's sentiment, I believe he's reversing the order that Scripture gives. Unsurprisingly, Morgan argues for inclusivism at best and relativism at worst.[19]

THE FINAL APOLOGETIC

Apologetics is not a field in and of itself. Cornelius Van Til posited that it's the discipline that runs through the entirety of Christian thought.[20] To some extent, everything we do as Christians in our words and our works concerns apologetics. Our aim in apologetics is to help believers worship God better.

According to Schaeffer, our "final apologetic" is love—not some abstract, ambiguous love, but the love demonstrated in John 17:21.[21] This love is manifested in believers' unity, which they then share with unbelievers. Apologetics combines the best of our thinking with the kindness of our hearts, both of which Christ has changed. Schaeffer states, "If this is not our own response first of all, and then the response of those whom we try to help, we have made a mistake somewhere."[22]

Our responsibility in ministry is to present believers mature in Christ (Colossians 1:28). As a result, we should help students formulate and defend their worldviews and, in doing so, expand their potential for worship to God (Ephesians 3:18).

My encouragement, in conclusion, is two-fold. First, I hope that youth workers will continue articulating and defending the Christian faith. May we never lose sight of the importance in helping students verbalize their beliefs.

Second, I hope that youth workers will expand their efforts. Advocating for a more holistic apologetic for students will require more time and energy, but it will also be more rewarding. It will demand that we respect the honest questions of teenagers about various issues and help them to understand what's behind them. My prayer is that by expanding our aims in youth ministry we might see more students embrace a more robust understanding of their faith.

REMODELING TIP

A tilt is needed in apologetics within most youth ministries. Evidence for Christianity, whether it's in the realm of archeology, history, or science, should be utilized in equipping Christian teens to defend their faith. However, from my observation, the early Christians, and indeed the Bible itself, models the presuppositional approach called for in this chapter. In the final charge, Chris urges that we should "respect the honest questions of teenagers about various issues and help them to understand what's behind them."

A teenager in our church recently sent me an email with this question: "So I've heard two contradicting views on sin. I've heard that some are worse than others, but I've also heard that all sins are equal. I mean, yes, I know murder and lying are both sins, but are they necessarily equal? Logically, I would think murdering the person (versus bad mouthing them) would be worse. Do you have any Scripture that would clear this up for me?"

Behind this basic question is the pop culture view of sin that's regrettably prevalent within much of the church. But it's a great question. And I told her so, because I certainly don't think we should chide students when they ask honest questions. Also, we shouldn't just give them answers. We should help them learn how to think through these types of issues and to fill in the gaps where their own worldview may be inconsistent.

- **Barry Raper,** Program Coordinator for Ministry Studies, Welch College, Gallatin, Tennessee

---

Discussion Questions

1. What is apologetics?
2. What is the difference between evidential and presuppositional apologetics?
3. How does apologetics differ from evangelism?
4. What is the "final apologetic"?
5. What must come before believing the gospel?
6. How do we relate our apologetics to our worldview? How do we relate apologetics to the worldviews of others?

Helpful Resources

Mark Coppenger, *Moral Apologetics for Contemporary Christians: Pushing Back Against Cultural and Religious Critics*, B&H Studies in Christian Ethics (Nashville: B&H, 2011).

Steven B. Cowan, ed., *Five Views on Apologetics* (Grand Rapids, Mich.: Zondervan, 2000).

"Keeping Our Kids, Part 1," *White Horse Inn Podcast*, May 18,

2014; http://www.whitehorseinn.org/blog/2014/05/18/whi-1206-keeping-our-kids-part-1/; accessed December 10, 2016. Internet.

"Keeping Our Kids, Part 2," *White Horse Inn Podcast*, May 25, 2015; http://www.whitehorseinn.org/blog/2014/05/25/whi-1207-keeping-our-kids-part-2/; accessed December 10, 2016; Internet.

C. S. Lewis, *Mere Christianity* (New York: HarperCollins, 1980).

Francis A. Schaeffer, *The Francis A. Schaeffer Trilogy* (Wheaton, Ill.: Crossway, 1990).

Vern Sheridan Poythress, *Inerrancy and Worldview: Answering Modern Challenges to the Bible* (Wheaton, Ill.: Crossway, 2012).

Larry Alex Taunton, "Listening to Young Atheists: Lessons for a Stronger Christianity," *The Atlantic*, June 6, 2013; http://www.theatlantic.com/national/archive/2013/06/listening-to-young-atheists-lessons-for-a-stronger-christianity/276584/; accessed September 14, 2015; Internet.

CHAPTER 7

FAMILY DISCIPLESHIP IN CHURCH AND HOME

"Every Christian family ought to be as it were a little church, consecrated to Christ, and wholly influenced and governed by his rules."

- JONATHAN EDWARDS[1]

The Christian faith is no stranger to family. After all, we walk into church to greet Brother so-and-so and his wife Sister so-and-so, even though we can't trace any biological heritage to these close Christian friends. The reason is that the gospel connects Christians in such profound ways that they can be described only in familial terms.

When Jesus was alerted to the presence of His mother and brothers during His public teaching, He pointed to His disciples, saying, "Here are my mother and my brothers! For whoever does the will of my Father in heaven is my brother and sister and mother" (Matthew 12:49-50).

The apostle Paul expands on this theme, addressing the church as a "household" or "family of God" (1 Timothy 3; 5:1-2; Titus 2:1-5). He tells believers to respect fathers and mothers in the faith and to treat one another as brothers and sisters in Christ. Both John and Paul see themselves as fathers in the faith to younger believers (1 Corinthians 4:16; 1 Timothy 1:2, 1 John 2:14; 3:18; 5:21).[2]

Within my own denomination, familial, or generational, discipleship has received a renewed focus thanks to the D6 movement. The aim of this ministry is to reemphasize the parental responsibility of spiritual formation. Deuteronomy 6:7-9 states:

> You shall teach them [God's Word] diligently to your children, and shall talk of them when you sit in your house, and when you walk by the way, and when you lie down, and when you rise. You shall bind them as a sign on your hand, and they shall be as frontlets between your eyes. You shall write them on the doorposts of your house and on your gates.

Even in the New Testament, Paul instructs parents and children (Ephesians 6:1-4). As stated before, and often overlooked, is that both of these commands are given within the context of the faith community.[3] When Moses gave this command to parents, he was explaining it to a gathering of the Israelites. When Paul instructed the families in Ephesus, the entire church read his letter.

Couching the community of faith in these terms might muddle our understanding of our earthly families. Does our faith family negate God's plan for spiritual formation from our nuclear families? When church becomes family, does family cease to be family? Or vice versa, when the family becomes church, does the gathering of believers become null and void? This ought not be the case, though imbalance can easily occur

For centuries, the Christian tradition has held that the Christian family and church are deeply connected in God's redemptive plan. For the believer, the church is family, and the family ought to be church. Of course, that doesn't mean that the church and the family are synonymous. Actually, these divine institutions are distinct in many ways, each accomplishing tasks that the other can't.

Rather, the church and the family are partners in spiritual formation, running alongside one another. As one author notes, "This two-fold approach is the foundation for comprehensive faith-at-home ministry—ministry that coordinates the God-ordained function of the Christian household with the church's role as a Christian's first family."[4] In this chapter, I aim to show how these two spheres are knitted together and are vital in the spiritual formation of the Christian child.

FAMILY AS CHURCH

Toward a Theology of Family

We must begin by understanding what God intended when He created the family. First, God ordained the family before the fall. This means that the family was an institution created before sin wrecked the world. Andreas Köstenberger offers this definition of family: "Primarily one man and one woman united in matrimony plus natural or adopted children and, secondarily, any other persons related by blood."[5]

This definition is reinforced and rooted in the familial models of the Old and New Testaments.

Second, the Christian family continues to accomplish God's redemptive work in this world like no other institution can. The family holds a singular position in God's will. Consider, for a moment, what Vigen Guroian writes concerning the parent-child relationship:

> In our day hyper-individualism and exaggerated notions of personal autonomy flourish culturally and have influenced law. The religious sociologist Robert Bellah calls this ontological individualism—a belief that the individual is primary and that the individual's claims take precedence over community, which is thought to be derivative and artificial. This individualism is reflected conspicuously in current attitudes and opinions about marriage and divorce, abortion, and physician-assisted suicide, to name a few. . . . To the extent that these notions of individualism and autonomy influence contemporary thought on childhood, there is a tendency to define childhood apart from serious reflection on the meaning of parenthood. Yet a moment's pause might lead one to recognize that *there is hardly a deeper characteristic of human life than the parent-child relationship*. . . . The Christian faith would have us look more closely at the fundamental parent-child nexus.[6]

Guroian notes the profound effect that parents have on their children. Aside from the husband-wife relationship, no relationship is more influential in all of culture than that of the parent-child.

Rarely can any other relationship cultivate the countercultural values important for life than the parent-child relationship. In *Family-based Youth Ministry*, Mark DeVries notes, "No one has more long-term interest in the students I work with than their parents do. . . . Families exert unparalleled influence on the development of the children's lives and character."[7] This isn't just a pragmatic statement; it's a theological one. God intended for families to have more influence on their children than any other variable.

Family Worship

What is the primary way by which a family can be a "little church"? The answer: by worshipping together. This isn't simply a solution to a problem; actually, family worship has its roots in Scripture. Abraham, Job, Moses, Joshua, Paul, and Peter all practiced or else referred to families worshipping together. A thread runs throughout Scripture that encourages parents and children to honor God together. In addition, this thread runs throughout Christian history.

The Free Will Baptist Church Covenant reads, "We agree faithfully to discharge our obligations in reference to the study of the Scriptures, secret prayer, *family devotions*, and social worship; and by self-denial, faith, and good works endeavor to 'grow in grace and the knowledge of our Lord and Saviour Jesus Christ.'"[8]

Family worship doesn't have to be complicated; parents need to remember that. We shouldn't be overwhelmed by the prospect of worshipping with our families. Donald

Whitney plainly encourages, "Just read, pray, and sing." Reading a passage of Scripture is simple enough. For those with younger children, you may choose a storybook Bible or a smaller passage that's appropriate for their age. Simply read through the passage or story together and make a few comments on what it means. As children get older, deal with heavier and lengthier passages.

Concerning prayer, use the biblical passage you've already read to lead your prayer. Pray whatever the application might be from a given biblical story. Further, allow family members to offer different prayer requests. Finally, have a hymnbook handy, or sing memorable Christian songs. It doesn't have to be all eight stanzas, but sing a song worshipfully with your family. Often times, this can be the most enjoyable moment for children.[9]

Simply by reading, praying, and singing together, you've worshipped with your family. This is easy to teach others and easy to practice yourself. Try to do this as often as possible. If you're able to do it every day, that's great! If not, at least try to keep a consistent schedule.

REMODELING TIP

Erin began attending youth group with her best friend, Hope, whose family attended our church. The girls were nearly inseparable, so Erin quickly made friends and felt at home. Through the faithful teaching of the gospel and a few key retreats, Erin began demonstrating fruit that she had become a Christian.

Erin's family periodically gave her grief that she was changing too much. Occasionally, they were even skeptical that we were brainwashing her. Since she was changing for the better, though, they continued to allow her to come. One summer during a missions trip, Erin's faith sunk in deep and her love for Jesus became contagious. As she began to speak more about her relationship with Christ, her family began to wonder more at the change in her life.

I wish I could say I played a more active role in discipling Erin, but that's simply not true. Instead, I credit Hope's family. Because the girls were friends, Erin spent much time around Hope's family: watching them interact, participating in their family conversations, and observing what a Christian family looks like. Hope's parents were never pushy, but they cared for Erin and showed great hospitality. A few years later, a similar pattern repeated itself with Hope's and Erin's younger siblings, who were also best friends with each other.

Examples like this illustrate how parents can function as youth pastors to their children's friends. This doesn't need to be complicated or intimidating: Show care and hospitality. As much as you're able, give the parents in your ministry a vision for the Great Commission by showing hospitality and intentional Christ-like care in their home for their kids' friends.

- **Mike McGarry,** Pastor of Youth and Family, Emmanuel Baptist Church, Norfolk, Virginia

---

Generational Discipleship

Family discipleship goes a step further; it's more than family worship, though that's vital. Family discipleship also occurs in more informal moments. One author notes, "Responsible youth ministry in the church, though perhaps difficult to execute, is simple to understand: it involves teaching and exhorting parents to raise their children biblically."[10]

Christian living must be both *verbalized* and *visualized* for our children. Parents should teach their children the propositional truths of Scripture, yes, but they must also live it out. Look for teachable moments to show how Christian truth applies in that situation. If you're a ministry leader, encourage other parents to do the same. This may occur during drives to school, when your child is having difficulty in organized sports, or around the dinner table. The possibilities are endless.

We've considered the Bible's instruction concerning the nuclear family. However, family ministry doesn't stop there. While we may experience the most wonderful family worship in between the four walls of our homes, we're missing an important component if our families aren't integrated into the life of the church.

CHURCH AS FAMILY

The church, the family of God, is a second institution in our family ministry paradigm. DeVries writes, "Only the church and the family can provide Christian nurture from birth to old age—even death. Almost all other groups students are involved in are essentially orphaning structures, including para-church youth ministries, schools, scouts *and youth groups*."[11]

This truth doesn't mean that we denigrate youth groups. Instead, it shows that youth groups aren't ultimately as powerful or as enduring as the family or the church, both of which God has ordained. They're communities through which God intends for us to become disciples. Therefore, as we seek to formulate our understanding of family ministry, these two institutions must remain primary.

The Family of God

"But when the fullness of time had come, God sent forth his Son, born of woman, born under the law, to redeem those who were under the law," Paul writes in Galatians, "so that we might receive adoption as sons. And because you are sons, God has sent the Spirit of his Son into our hearts, crying, 'Abba! Father!' So you are no longer a slave, but a son, and if a son, then an heir through God" (4:4-7).

For Christians, one of the best ways to describe our identity is as sons and daughters of God. In a manner, the church is the Christian's extended family of God. As one author notes, "The church has greater potential than any other institution for serving as an extended family for isolated nuclear families and singles. Yet few churches have effectively stepped into that role."[12]

To benefit fully from the connection between church and home, we must have a better understanding of the church-as-family. "The goal of church-as-family is to help God's people relate to one another like a family. What this means is that the church nurtures members within a rich matrix of multi-generational relationships," explains Timothy Paul Jones.[13]

Jones continues: "Children and teenagers whose parents aren't believers find their lives intertwined with mature men and women who become spiritual parents and grandparents. Married couples mentor singles. New parents learn child rearing from empty nesters. . . . Church-as-family ministry clearly recognizes that, inasmuch as I am a follower of Jesus, my family includes anyone who does the will of my heavenly father (Mark 3:35)."[14]

Church-as-family involves more than a parent discipling his or her child. Whereas family-as-church is generational discipleship, church-as-family encourages *inter*generational discipleship. Where generational discipleship consists of a parent discipling their child, intergenerational discipleship consists of the many generations within the church caring for and discipling a Christian child. The church is the glorious family of God, and thus discipleship occurs across all age groups, stages of life, and family makeups.

REMODELING TIP

The key to family discipleship is being intentional. Whether it's after ball games or church or before bed, discipleship can happen anywhere at any time. There are many ways to disciple students, but two stand out to me: (1) family worship service and (2) riding to church together as a family.

Students need age-based learning such as Sunday school and children's church because they need to learn with others their age. However, there's also a need for students to worship in church with their families. Parents can thus teach their children how to worship. Not only can their children observe them, but the children can also see that they belong in the church.

After service is over, families should also discuss what they heard in service, Sunday school, and small groups during the drive home. Church leadership could even provide families with questions or overviews so that parents can better disciple their children.

Students who don't have Christian parents will need spiritual adoptive parents, which might be a bus captain, grandparent, or some other mature Christian. Whoever brings that student to church can become their church parent. Spiritual adoptive parents should allow their children to sit with them during family worship, and they should also lead discussion during the drive home. This is extremely important because those students won't have the opportunity to worship as a family in the home.

Remember, students will have questions. Be happy if they're asking you questions. It's an opportunity to steer them toward God.

- **Nathan Peoples,** Student Pastor, Cramerton Free Will Baptist Church, Cramerton, North Carolina

---

Intergenerational Discipleship

One of the biggest concerns I have about many current family ministry models is the blind spot they can often create. If we're not careful, focusing on family ministry can cause us to fail to see those children who come from non-Christian homes.

This brings up a glaring question: How do we, in family ministry, disciple those who don't come from Christian homes? The answer is simple, though its implementation can be difficult. For those students who don't have a Christian family, the family of God becomes their family. In a manner, the church family adopts them in a way that encourages intergenerational discipleship. When this approach is embraced, the faith of even those who have been blessed with a Christian family will grow even more robust, as they too are surrounded by mature Christian mentors and friends.

However, this method calls for a paradigm shift in the way we think of youth ministry.[15] In this kind of ministry, the youth would no longer be separated from the adults and educated by a rogue youth pastor and his band of merry men (or volunteers). Instead, as DeVries notes, rather than being a "dangling appendage," the youth would instead be "at the center of a web, a convergent community connected not only to him or her but also to each other."[16]

Chap Clark has extrapolated much of what the church-as-family looks like, practically speaking, in his "adoptive" youth ministry paradigm.[17] While Clark, DeVries, and others have dealt with this paradigm more exhaustively, the average youth minister should note several important distinctions.

Each church deals with unique situations in its own

context. The local church must be careful, in consideration of liability risks, in determining how intergenerational discipleship should look in their own area; a local church must be careful in protecting its children and people from harm. Nevertheless, as an example, church leaders can apply this model of discipleship through shepherding groups, parent-child activities, and intergenerational activities.

First, within the context of your youth group, you may start what some have called a "shepherding group." This is a smaller group of students who are mentored and cared for by an adult other than the youth leader, perhaps a volunteer or parent. Encourage this leader to spend time with these students outside of church, meeting with them and mentoring them.

Second, take the opportunity to have father-son and mother-daughter activities. At one church where I ministered, we had a father-son baseball game and a mother-daughter pottery night. Unexpectedly, the most wonderful thing happened. Those mothers who had only sons asked if they could "adopt" a girl in the youth group who didn't have parents involved in church for the pottery night, and vice versa for the fathers. Mature Christian parents "adopted" our students to spend quality time with them. You can imagine how much this meant to the students.

Lastly, you may start annual intergenerational activities. A favorite is to host a Thanksgiving dinner for elderly church members. Each student brings a side dish, and the church provides the turkey. While the food is good, the most poignant element is that students split up and sit with the older church members. Few activities, in my experience, have been more meaningful to both groups than this meal. The young students and older saints get to know each other on a deeper and more personal level.

YOUTH MINISTRY AS A BRIDGE

Noting the struggle that many youth ministers face, one author wrote, "We haven't found that silver bullet. While small groups, mentoring, justice work, and a host of other youth ministry programs are important, the reality is that the challenges of kids, ministry programs, and spiritual development are far too complicated to be met with a single solution. There's no cure-all."[18]

It's true. Not any one ministry solution will fix all of your problems. As the church and family work together, though, we can begin, when the gospel is central and Christ glorified, to see our students mature in their faith.

DeVries writes, "There is no such thing as successful youth ministry that isolates teenagers from the community of faith."[19] The key ingredients of any child's spiritual formation are a godly family and the family of God. It's not either/or but instead a both/and. The family needs the church, and the church needs the family.

When all is said and done, the youth ministry and its leadership are at the center of that relationship, able either to encourage and exhort or to distract and deter. The youth pastor is providentially placed in a position that ought to bridge the gap between the home and the church. For effective and biblical youth ministry, the youth pastor must make the most of this relationship, helping the church and home partner as they walk in tandem.

Discussion Questions

1. How might a church minister to those students who don't come from Christian families or homes?
2. What are some ways in which the church can practice "adoption" of the students in their youth ministry?
3. Why and how may a family worship together?
4. What is the difference between generational and intergenerational discipleship?
5. Who is the primary discipler of children: the family or the church?
6. How might we define the nuclear family from a biblical perspective?

Helpful Resources

Voddie Baucham, Jr., *Family Shepherds: Calling and Equipping Men to Lead Their Homes* (Wheaton, Ill.: Crossway, 2011).

Chap Clark, ed., *Adoptive Youth Ministry: Integrating Emerging Generations into the Family of Faith* (Grand Rapids, Mich.: Baker Academic, 2016).

Mark DeVries, *Family-based Youth Ministry*, rev. and exp. (Downers Grove, Ill.: Intervarsity, 2004).

Ron Hunter, Jr., *The DNA of D6: Building Blocks of Generational Discipleship* (Nashville: Randall House, 2015).

Andreas J. Köstenberger with David W. Jones, *God, Marriage, and the Family: Rebuilding the Biblical Foundation,* 2nd ed. (Wheaton, Ill.: Crossway, 2010).

Christopher Shlect, *Critique of Modern Youth Ministry,* 2nd ed. (Moscow, Ida.: Canon, 2007).

Donald S. Whitney, *Family Worship* (Wheaton, Ill.: Crossway, 2016).

PART III

BUILDING FOR THE FUTURE

CHAPTER 8

PREPARING FOR SUSTAINABLE CHANGE

"All we have to decide is what to do with the time that is given us."

- GANDALF[1]

Mark Twain allegedly said that babies with wet diapers are the only people who like change. Add that to the adage, "You can't even expect change from a vending machine," and we suddenly have the majority opinion on change, especially in ministry.

Virtually no one likes change in ministry, or at least they don't want you to change the things they like. Whether young or old, people like to keep their preferences the same, no matter how unhealthy or unbiblical they may be. Nevertheless, many pastors, and youth pastors in particular, find themselves in ministries that desperately need something to change. No matter if we're new to the church, or if we've been in charge of the youth group for decades, we're well aware that certain things need fixin'.

Within the first few weeks of full-time ministry, I decided to sit down and write out my philosophy of ministry.

I was excited about what the Lord could do in our youth group. I sat down at my computer to write out my thoughts. I picked a nice font, organized my views, and began typing away. I thought it looked great.

As though I had an epiphany, information flowed from my brain to my fingertips. Three essential principles for youth ministry emerged: (1) Gospel-driven, (2) Bible-saturated, and (3) Relational ministry. (In many ways, I don't think these have changed.) I even included my goals for youth ministry in those early months. In a rush, I attached this multi-page philosophy of ministry to an email and sent it to my volunteers.

While my volunteers agreed with everything I had put in that short position paper, and even though they wanted to see the same change occur in our ministry, not much happened immediately following my *magnum opus*. What did happen was slow, sustainable change over months and even years. Those first months revealed my naiveté concerning ministry leadership. If I taught and shared all the right principles, I thought, then our youth group would turn out perfect and grow immediately.

Of course, that's not how ministry always works. Even if we have the best intentions and know the right things, creating positive change in youth ministry can be very difficult.

"Change has a way of making or breaking youth ministry leaders, especially within their first two years. Some leaders boldly and blindly rearrange their ministry regardless of people's responses. Others are paralyzed by the thought of suggesting change because they fear negative reactions," explains Doug Fields. "You have no easy, magic-formula, works-every-time procedure to implement change, but you can take some take some definitive actions to minimize conflict."[2]

I agree with Fields. There's no silver bullet that's going to allow you to implement change in a perfect, stress-free manner. At the same time, we can approach change in either healthy or unhealthy ways in our quest for change. In this chapter, I will consider two components that will enable the youth leader to bring about the needed change in his youth ministry.

SOLID FOUNDATION

The first component required for change in youth ministry is a solid foundation. This may seem obvious, but it's often overlooked and forgotten about. Why are we just considering this issue now? A youth leader can't steer his youth ministry in the right direction if he hasn't first dealt with the fundamental issues and principles of ministry. Fields argues, "Most of the arguments in youth ministry aren't about theology; they're about change."[3]

I understand Fields's sentiment, but I wouldn't draw so sharp a contrast between the two. As we saw in chapter two, theology and methodology, or theology and change, are linked to one another. So, before even thinking about change, we must ensure that our foundation is solid

Semper Reformanda, sola Scriptura, and *ad fontes* are three Latin phrases from the Reformation that give us this solid foundation. (Also, now that you know Latin, you can impress all of your friends at parties.) First, much of

Protestantism has held to the principle of *semper Reformanda*, which means "always reforming." The church, and for our purposes youth ministry, must constantly seek reformation, or change, in specific ways. The crucial question, of course, is what we should reform

This is where the second phrase comes in to play. During the Reformation, the church articulated five *solas*: (1) *sola Scriptura*, meaning "Scripture alone"; (2) *sola fide*, meaning "faith alone"; (3) *sola gratia*, meaning "grace alone"; (4) *solo Christo*, meaning "Christ alone"; and (5) *soli Deo Gloría*, meaning "to God alone be the glory."

While each of these *solas* is necessary for youth ministry, *sola Scriptura* is an especially important foundation. We should continually fold the edges of our youth ministries back in toward what the Bible says. We must hold the Bible up as a mirror to our ministries, always asking whether our practices line up with it.

Mark Senter notes the impact of Scripture on students' lives: "Students who value the Bible will have a willingness to receive biblical truth, respond by being obedient to Scripture, value opportunities to discover more about God's Word, organize their activities so that contact with the Bible is frequent, and ultimately are characterized as being people who have been transformed into fully devoted followers of Christ."[4]

Is this not what we want for all of our students? By depending on the Bible, we're showing everyone involved in our ministries that we believe in the sufficiency of Scripture. This is the only infallible, inerrant, solid foundation for which we can hope

Finally, we must go *ad fontes*, meaning, literally, "to the fountains." This term was used frequently during the Renaissance when artists, authors, scientists, and others went back to the original sources in their studies.

This same dynamic also occurred during the Reformation. With the Roman Catholic Church giving more power to non-biblical authorities such as the pope, the Protestant reformers were calling the church back to the sources, back to the Bible and the early church. The Reformers believed that Scripture should have authority over the believer and the church.

For that reason, youth ministry should always look to the Bible. When we're wondering what needs to change, we must remember the basics, always checking our ideas against the Bible. The best way forward for your ministry is, in a sense, backward. Change fails in youth ministry because we lack a good foundation.

Too often, youth ministry is tempted by a moving target that proves a faulty foundation. Youth leaders try too hard to catch the next wave of trends. But what happens when that wave hits the shore and dissolves? Instead, our youth ministries should be built on a proper foundation rather than on shifting sands or dangerous waters.

ORGANIC CHANGE

In addition to having a solid foundation, we must also have organic change. Yet, if change is resisted, then how can it ever be organic? Change seems like the last thing that would happen naturally in our ministry contexts. However, if we want to make lasting change—changes that result in sustainable effectiveness—we must figure it out.

In *The Trellis and the Vine*, Colin Marshall and Tony Payne present the concept of organic versus non-organic elements of ministry. They draw a dichotomy between vine work, which is organic, and trellis work.

Vine work refers to "the basic work of any Christian ministry." It's the call to "preach the gospel of Jesus Christ in the power of God's Spirit, and to see people converted, changed and grow to maturity in that gospel. That's the work of planting, watering, fertilizing and tending the vine."[5] The organic side of ministry includes those elements that comprise our solid foundation—those non-negotiables that have been consistent throughout Church history.

Trellis work, on the other hand, refers to the structures in place so that the vine can grow well.[6] These include "management, finances, infrastructure, organization, [and] governance."[7] The trellis, though it's not organic, helps in the overall health of the ministry. The trellis can change, but the vine, in its essence, remains the same. Marshall and Payne call these the trellis and the vine.

While not identical to Marshall and Payne's presentation, Mark DeVries offers the dichotomy of architecture and atmosphere for sustainable youth ministry. Architecture refers to the structure, whereas atmosphere refers to "the culture, climate and ethos that sustains the health of an organization."[8]

The problem that arises in ministry is that so many ministry leaders focus either on one side or the other. Architecture or trellis work can easily take over our ministries.

While important, it's not the primary reason we're in ministry. We're in ministry to grow fruit. In order to find a healthy order, we should focus on sustainability in leadership and ministry.

Sustainable Leadership

For leadership to be sustainable, it must be able to continue for the long-term. This isn't an easy task, especially in youth ministry. In fact, sustainability is near impossible in view of the fact that the average tenure of a youth minister is about eighteen months.[9] How can you create a culture that is long-term oriented when statistics are fighting against you? Even more, how do you create change, which sounds antithetical to sustainability, if you want to stay around?

Although long-term sustainability and effective change might seem at odds, nothing could be further from the truth. Actually, long-term commitment in leadership is necessary to create change that's healthy for your ministry. Although many youth ministers make growing student leaders their goal, or at least to give students an opportunity to lead, this is all null and void if the youth pastor isn't a good leader. Good student leadership can be kingdom-effective, but youth pastors must be committed to sustainable leadership

Sustainable leadership will require both character and consistency. First, character is of the utmost importance in leadership. The youth pastor must be a man of holiness and integrity. The Bible requires calls of God's leaders to exhibit personal integrity (Titus 1:5-9; 1 Timothy 3:1-7; 1 Peter 5:1-4).

"Your character is not only the foundation your ministry will be built upon, it's also the garden of life from which the fruit of ministry will continually grow," explains David Schroeder, speaking on the importance of character in youth ministry. "In other words, the expression of your gifts and skills in ministry must always be fueled by the increasing depth of your character. If not, one day your tank will run dry, and your skills will not sustain you. Some have imploded for this very reason."[10]

Growth in character isn't simply for our spiritual growth, although that's important. Actually, it's required if our students themselves are going to grow in the gospel. Josh Branum writes,

> Student ministers must constantly proclaim the truth of the gospel to their people, but if their lives contradict their message by a lack of holiness, the message loses its appeal. . . . Rather than being known solely for their ability to organize programs or utilize relevant illustrations in their sermons, student ministers should primarily be known as examples of godliness, submission, and devotion. Those who proclaim the life-changing gospel of Jesus Christ publicly must strive not to contradict that same message privately. In fact, it is of the utmost importance that student ministers reinforce the gospel message by gospel centered living.[11]

Character—personal holiness—is indispensable for leading youth groups. Leaders can't lead where they haven't been.

If we want our students to plumb the depths of the Christian faith, then we too must have plumbed those depths.

The second component of sustainable leadership is consistency. Undoubtedly, this overlaps with character. With such a high turnover rate, as well as unfortunate caricatures of youth leaders, showing consistency in youth ministry can be quite difficult. People want to know that those in charge of their kids are reliable and responsible.

The question, then, is how we combat the pre-conceived notions that people have about youth ministry. DeVries notes that youth ministry "may be one of the only professions that has settled into the pattern of handing over total responsibility for running an organization to young people just out of college."[12] DeVries is right.

At the same time, we can take certain steps to demonstrate responsibility. Make an extra effort to communicate to your parents and volunteers. Fight against the "maverick youth pastor" persona. Respond to emails within twenty-four hours. Stop mudding in the church van. You get the idea.

While this advice may sound counter-intuitive, a mentor of mine once said, "Even though you're in your twenties, act like you are in your forties." The basic idea was this: Exhibit responsibility that's currently beyond my years. Break the mold of what people expect out of you. In doing so, people will begin to respect your leadership and trust you with your ministry.

Sustainable Ministry

So far, we've tackled the leadership component of organic change. In addition, we must consider how the ministry itself can be sustained. That can be a difficult task because so much is involved in the day-to-day upkeep of any one ministry. Youth pastors eat lunch with kids, meet up for coffee to disciple, chat with parents after church, teach Bible lessons, and coordinate small groups. With everything going on, pursuing sustainable change can be challenging.

You may not like this, but I believe that positive change in ministry can be summed up in one word: slow. If you want your ministry to experience healthy change, the best path forward is a slow, consistent, sustainable one. This doesn't mean that some things don't need to be changed right away. Some practices should be reformed immediately, such as false teaching.

However, the majority of changes will probably need time. Ron Hunter writes, "If you want change to last, don't rush it. You can change environments rather quickly, but you change cultures over time."[13] Hunter is exactly right. If we want the culture of our church, or the ethos of our ministry, to change, we must invest time and dedication.

I love how DeVries explains this principle: "Sustainable change happens when leaders recognize the power of incremental revolution, the power of one small change after another, until the incremental changes result in exponential change."[14] Healthy change is often more like baby steps than one giant leap.

The apostle Paul shows this kind of growth in the life of the believer. Remember how he described the works of the Christian life as the fruit of the Spirit. Think about it: Paul could have used anything to demonstrate these virtues of the Christian life. He could have referred to them as the elements or steps or blocks of the Spirit. But he didn't.

Writing under the inspiration of the Holy Spirit, Paul used the image of organic fruit. Virtues like love, joy, peace, forbearance, kindness, goodness, faithfulness, gentleness, and self-control, more often than not, grow within us slowly yet strongly.

Although we might increase the speed of the growth process through performance-enhancing drugs, such efforts are unhealthy, resulting in long-term harm to the person using them. In the same way, you can use quick, easy shortcuts to grow your ministry. Yet they'll usually result in long-term harm to you and your students. Because of this, pursue health in your ministry. Seek to grow your youth group by God's provision and guidance. After all, Christ did say, "*I* will build my Church" (Matthew 16:18).[15]

REMODELING TIP

As a youth pastor going into my first ministry, I observed the need for change everywhere. I wanted to save the day; I wanted to save the youth and the church. However, trying to build a youth praise band and to give our teenagers their own meeting room didn't go as expected. Having students who couldn't play instruments and having to share a room with an adult class wasn't what I envisioned. Dealing with leadership boards and committees was also frustrating. I felt as if my hands were tied.

My second youth ministry began about the same as my first—slow. Although I was impatient, and we weren't going anywhere fast, parents and students would often come by and thank me for what I was doing. That was confusing at first because I didn't think I was doing anything.

Over time I watched my ministries begin to take shape. They began to resemble what I had hoped they would from the beginning. Eventually, students who were in band at school began to play at church too. I was even given a classroom, just for my teenagers.

The key to positive change in your ministry is longevity. I think it takes four to five years minimum for you to feel as if it's your youth group. After being at a church for an extended period, you develop relationships that go beyond teenagers and class time. You get to know them, their families, the church, and the leadership. God uses these times to make your youth ministry His youth ministry. You're just along for the ride.

- Darren Walker, Associate Youth and Children's Pastor, First Free Will Baptist Church, Washington, North Carolina

---

CONCLUSION

I've never said, and I will never say, that youth ministry is easy. "Want to build a ministry that lasts, a ministry that deeply impacts students, families and the wider world? Then be prepared for the mess."[16] It's hard work—but it's worth it! It's worth the toil and struggle, the heartbreak and headaches. It's woefully messy, but when you're committed to Christ and His church, He'll see you through. God will give you the grace and strength to accomplish what He has called you to do.

Ministry isn't glamorous, as Tim Schmoyer reminds us: "Real ministry is not as glamorous as it seems. Real ministry is messy. It's about getting into sticky areas of depraved lives and doing whatever's necessary to encourage growth and maturity. When it requires confrontation, it's very difficult, awkward, and stressful. This is not glamorous at all."[17]

At the same time, we shouldn't assume that it's glamorous. God give us His goals for us. Ours is to decide what to do with them. Focus on the primary things in your leadership: your character and consistency. Focus on the primary things in your ministry, seeking to follow God's truth to the best of your ability. Little bit by little bit, you'll begin to see amazing, powerful, sustainable change occur in your youth ministry.

Discussion Questions

1. What are the necessary elements for sustainable leadership? Why?
2. What are some ways in which change can be unhealthy?
3. What's the best way to approach sustainable ministry? Why?
4. How does Paul describe change in the Christian life? How does that affect our understanding of ministry?
5. What does consistency look like in a youth pastor's life?
6. In what ways can we build a solid foundation for change? Is there anything you would add?

Helpful Resources

Josh Branum, "Personal Holiness and Evangelistic Leadership: Understanding the Relationship Between Practicing Spiritual Disciplines and Effective Student Evangelism," *The Journal of Youth Ministry*, vol. 15, no. 1 (Fall 2016).

Mark DeVries, ed., *Letters to a Youth Worker* (Brentwood, Tenn.: Center for Youth Ministry Training, 2012).

Mark DeVries, *Sustainable Youth Ministry: Why Most Youth Ministry Doesn't Last and What Your Church Can Do About It* (Downers Grove, Ill.: InterVarsity, 2008).

Doug Fields, *Your First Two Years in Youth Ministry: A Personal and Practical Guide to Starting Right* (Grand Rapids, Mich.: Zondervan, 2002).

Colin Marshall and Tony Payne, *The Trellis and the Vine: The Ministry Mind-Shift That Changes Everything* (Kingsford, NSW, Australia: Matthias Media, 2009).

CHAPTER 9

TEACHING TEENS

"God's Word is the most powerful force in the universe."

- JONATHAN LEEMAN[1]

Often I hear youth pastors say something like, "I'm a youth pastor, so I don't preach." If you're a pastor—of any flavor—your primary responsibility is to teach and preach the Word (1 Timothy 4:13; 2 Timothy 4:2-4; 2:15-16; James 3:1). Even more, today's youth are among the groups of people who are *most* in need of a steady diet of Scripture.

In a world of mixed messages, the Bible stands as students' authoritative guide for faith and practice. While students can receive the Word in a variety of ways, one of the most transformative (not to mention biblically commanded) is by hearing it proclaimed publicly in the presence of other believers.[2] Students *need* to hear their pastor teach and preach the Bible to them. And they need to hear it in presence of their peers so that they can hold each other accountable.

To teach teenagers effectively, we must combine the best of our youth ministry philosophy with effective communication. This means that we should allow topics such as these to inform the way we understand and instruct teenagers: the *missio Dei,* apologetics, ecclesiology, biblical theology, and a theology of culture and technology, among others. It means studying both the Bible and our culture with diligence.

Biblical and cultural exegesis is hard work. In a sense, it's the most difficult task for the youth minister—it can seem impossible. We might feel as though we could never know or study enough to feel adequate. But we can't lose hope. It's a serious challenge, but it's not impossible.

This chapter will offer helpful instructions for youth ministers to teach their teenagers effectively. This won't make you a perfect teacher, but I hope it will make you a biblical one. In some ways, much of this book culminates on this point.

This chapter is informed largely by the discipline of homiletics, or the art and practice of preaching. Concerning the proclamation of God's truth, books on homiletics are hard to beat. Thus, while I'll make occasional reference to youth ministry texts, I'll appeal more to those influential volumes on preaching. Although teaching and preaching are, in some sense, distinct, they also overlap significantly.

BRIDGE-BUILDING

We youth ministers are "between two worlds," as John Stott's classic title posits.[3] We stand between the ancient, transcendent truths of Scripture and the ever-changing, present world. Bad teaching is usually found in a break of this balance. Stott writes, "It is across this broad and deep divide of two thousand years of changing culture (more still in the case of the Old Testament) that Christian communicators have to throw bridges. Our task is to enable God's revealed truth to flow out of the Scriptures into the lives of the men and women today."[4]

Even beyond the gulf of time, building bridges is difficult. There are myriad barriers such as language, customs, and culture, which differ from what we see in the Bible. Biblical communicators will often swing toward one extreme. Some dive deep into Scripture but forget the magnificent relevance of God's Word. Such speakers end up presenting exegetical papers to their students; they decipher the ancient languages and the Bible's theology, but they don't often make sense of it practically.

Other communicators focus so much on the relevance of today's world that they forget God's transcendence, Scripture's depth, and the church's history. They forget careful interpretation of the biblical text, thus failing to rightly handle the Word of truth (2 Timothy 2:15). This error is probably more common among youth ministers.

To teach teenagers effectively, we must hold both these worlds in tandem and bring them together. This is why I like Gregory Carlson's definition of biblical teaching, which he states should put "one hand on the student [and] the other on the Word of God, bringing them together for life change."[5] Thus, we're not taking students to the ancient world, or bringing the ancient world to students. Rather, we're seeking to bring them together.

GOD'S (ANCIENT) TRUTH

Numerous books offer helpful ways to work through a biblical passage in preparation for teaching. Lawrence Richards and Gary Bredfeldt created and shared the Hook, Book, Look, and Took method.[6] This includes getting the students' attention, clarifying the meaning of the passage, understanding the implications, and finally showing the student how he or she should respond to the passage. This is the method that I often encourage my youth ministry students to use.

Doug Fields and Duffy Robbins implemented the acronym S.T.I.C.K. (Study, Think, Illustrate, Construct, and Keep Focused) to teach teenagers.[7] This method does well to keep focusing on the passage throughout the entire process.

Authorial Intent

Whatever process you choose to follow, the careful handling of Scripture should be consistent. This can be accomplished by following the basics of biblical interpretation: (1) observation, (2) interpretation, and (3) application. The majority of methods already make room for this in their process. Interpretation is the heart of any teaching or preaching preparation.

As you walk through these three steps, you're essentially asking three major questions: First, you should ask, "What's there?" Observe the passage and ensure that you have a clear understanding of what's included.

Second, you should ask, "What does the passage mean?" Make sense of the passage. See if anything doesn't make sense, and try to clarify any difficulties. Find the basic meaning in the passage at this step. Lastly, you should ask, "How can the passage be lived out in the lives of your teenagers?" In other words, apply the passage. Be specific.[8]

If we haven't interpreted a passage right, we'll make a wreck of our sermon or lesson. As you walk through interpreting the passage, make clear that "God chose to reveal Himself within history to nations that can be located on a map," as Haddon Robinson explains. "These nations were enveloped in cultures as developed as our own. They used languages that can be described in grammars. We must first try to understand what the revelation of God meant for the men and women to whom it was originally given."[9]

Moreover, make sure that you're finding the original meaning of the passage. This refers to what the original author, whether Moses or Micah or Paul or Peter or whoever, intended for their original audience. Sometimes this comes easy because the author is explicit. For example, John writes, "I write these things to you who believe in the name of the Son of God, that you may know that you have eternal life" (1 John 5:13). Other passages can be more difficult. Whatever the challenges, we must work to the best of our ability to seek the original meaning of a passage.

Seeking the original meaning stands against the more popular reader-response theory of interpretation. Reader-response criticism places meaning not in the author's intentions but in the reader's reactions. A given passage could mean as many things as there are readers.

In contrast to this, we should seek to understand and teach the Bible according to the intended meaning of its authors, which includes not simply the human authors but ultimately the divine author, God Himself. We should all seek that intended meaning(s) rather than imposing some meaning contrary to its intention.

Christ-centered

As mentioned in chapter four, we must tell the whole story of Scripture, which begins and ends with Christ. He is in both the first and last chapters of the Bible: "I will put enmity between you and the woman, and between your offspring and her offspring; *he* shall bruise your head, and you shall bruise his heel" (Genesis 3:15); and, "The grace of the Lord Jesus be with all. Amen" (Revelation 22:21). He is also in every chapter in-between. The Christ is the axis on which the entire Bible turns. Ultimately, each book speaks to His centrality.

"The key to preaching the gospel every time," explains Tim Keller, "is to preach Christ every time, and the key to that is to find how your particular text fits into the full canonical context and participates as a chapter in the great narrative arc of the Bible, which is how God saves us and renews the world through the salvation by free grace in His Son, Jesus Christ."[10]

At the same time, we must be careful not to spiritualize or allegorize the passage we're teaching or preaching in a fashion contrary to the Bible's intentions. We're not looking for a *sensus plenior,* or deeper meaning, behind the text.

That's why we should apply a historical-grammatical approach to our interpretation of a passage while also being faithful to that grand story of the Bible. We're not simply imagining or shoehorning Christ into every passage that we preach. Instead, we're using a Christocentric hermeneutic. We believe that God inspired all Scripture through the Holy Spirit, by which He intended to unfold the great plan of redemption (2 Timothy 3:16-17; Hebrews 1:1-2; 2 Peter 1:20-21).

While not all passages speak of Christ equally, some being more explicit than others, they all contribute to God's great "promise plan."[11] For this reason, we want our sermons and lessons to be specifically Christian. What does each passage say about the person and work of Christ or about God's redemptive plan? What would keep a Muslim imam or Jewish rabbi from preaching the same message? We want to teach and preach more than moralism; we want to "preach Christ crucified" (1 Corinthians 1:23).

THE (CONTEMPORARY) WORLD

We're not working simply between the two worlds, though. Robinson adds a third: "Expositors must be involved in three different worlds: the world of the Bible, the modern world, and the particular world in which we are called to preach."[12]

The youth pastor, then, needs to be aware of two spheres, one concentrically placed within the other. First, the youth pastor should recognize the macro-societal subjects at play, the first and larger sphere. This includes, but is not limited to, the arts, economics, education, government, law, the sciences, and vocation. These are the broad, big categories of our society that affect how we do the smaller things. Abraham Kuyper referred to these as the "spheres of life."[13]

While the task is big, you as the youth pastor should seek to understand how the Bible informs all of these areas of life. As Kuyper himself reminded us, "There is not a square inch in the whole domain of our human existence over which Christ, who is Sovereign over all, does not cry, Mine!"[14] If this is true, and I believe it is, then we need to be aware of how the Bible applies in the intricate details of life. For those seeking to understand the broader issues of culture, I recommend any of the following books:

- Bruce Ashford, *Every Square Inch: An Introduction to Cultural Engagement for Christians* (Bellingham, Wash.: Lexham, 2015).
- Craig Detweiler, *iGods: How Technology Shapes Our Spiritual and Social Lives* (Grand Rapids, Mich.: Brazos, 2013).
- Greg Forster, *Joy for the World* (Wheaton, Ill.: Crossway, 2014).
- Russell Moore, *Onward: Engaging the Culture Without Losing the Gospel* (Nashville: B&H, 2015).
- Ken Myers, *All God's Children and Blue Suede Shoes* (Wheaton, Ill.: Crossway, 1989).
- Vern Poythress, *Redeeming Science* (Wheaton, Ill.: Crossway, 2006).
- Hans Rookmaaker, *Modern Art and the Death of a Culture* (Wheaton, Ill.: Crossway, 1970).
- Kenman Wong and Scott Rae, *Business for the Common Good: A Christian Vision for the Marketplace* (Downers Grove, Ill.: InterVarsity, 2011).

Second, the youth pastor should be aware of his own, local circumstances. How does your community differ from others? How is your ministry or your group of students different from the church down the road, or across the state or country? What is youth culture? Although this chapter doesn't allow an exhaustive exposition of teen culture, I recommend the following:

- Dean Borgman, *Hear My Story: Understanding the Cries of Troubled Youth* (Peabody, Mass.: Hendrickson, 2003).
- Chap Clark, *Hurt 2.0: Inside the World of Today's Teenagers* (Grand Rapids, Mich.: Baker Academic, 2011).
- Kenda Creasy Dean, *Almost Christian: What the Faith of Our Teenagers Is Telling the American Church* (New York: Oxford University Press, 2010).
- David Kinnaman with Aly Hawkins, *You Lost Me: Why Young Christians Are Leaving the Church . . . and Rethinking the Faith* (Grand Rapids, Mich.: Baker, 2011).
- Walt Mueller, *Engaging the Soul of Youth Culture: Bridging Teen Worldviews and Christian Truth* (Downers Grove, Ill.: IVP, 2006).
- Walt Mueller, *Youth Culture 101* (El Cajon, Calif.: Zondervan, 2007).
- Rob and Amy Reinow, *Five Reasons for Spiritual Apathy in Teens: What Parents Can Do To Help* (Nashville: Randall House, 2015)

- Merton P. Strommen, *Five Cries of Youth* (San Francisco: Harper & Row, 1988).[15]

To offer a few broad descriptions Mueller posits that the emerging generation has unique marks. Generally, they are without a moral compass, culturally diverse, pluralistic and tolerant, part of broken relationships, alienated, media-saturated, experience and feeling driven, suspicious of truth, overwhelmed by options, part of a globalized youth culture, pervaded by violence, materialistic, concerned with appearance, deeply spiritual, and crying out for redemption.[16]

These characteristics may shock and discourage us. In another sense, though, they remind us that today's students deal with the same basic problems that have plagued humanity from the Garden.[17] While the symptoms change, the problem and prognosis stay the same.

BROUGHT TOGETHER

Bringing these two (or three) worlds together is the most difficult part of all. How do we connect the two-thousand-year-old meaning of an ancient text to the tumultuous culture of our teenagers? In a sense, we do this by showing students that Christ is Lord over it all: the past and the present. Stott noted, "We have to provoke them to think about their life in all its moods, to challenge them to make Jesus Christ the Lord of every area of it, and to demonstrate his contemporary relevance."[18]

As we preach and teach on different subjects, we should continually remind our students that Christ is Lord over every part of it. This shows our students that Christ is not only important in the church (though He is) but also in their homes, schools, jobs, and relationships. This requires special attention to how we apply each passage, but it's profoundly impactful when done appropriately.

Another major way of accomplishing this is by reminding our students of one simple truth: God has spoken. As the title of Francis Schaeffer's book tells us, He is there, and He is not silent.[19] The fact that God has spoken in a clear, authoritative, sufficient manner changes the way we interact with the Bible. I remind my students all the time: When you open the Bible—whether for devotions, teaching or preaching, or whatever—you're partaking in a miracle.

The God of the universe has given you instruction through this book, and you can understand it. That is phenomenal, life-changing truth we must affirm to our students. We need to remind our students of how wondrous it is to hear from their Creator! Familiarity can easily breed contempt. Because of this, we should ensure that we ourselves are in awe of God's Word and allow that to overflow into the rest of our ministry.

REMODELING TIP

Teaching is essential for students. Not only do they need to know why they believe what they believe, but they truly want to know too. These truths can be found by digging deeply into God's Word and by teaching them how to have a personal relationship with Jesus Christ.

I used to be reluctant to teach the Old Testament, fearing that it would bore my students to death. Much to my surprise, I found that they actually loved it. It even helped them to understand the New Testament better.

Don't be mistaken. Not all teaching is done inside the four walls of the church. The relationships we build with our students give us the opportunity to teach spiritual truths through life lessons as well. True teaching takes work. It takes investing a part of our lives into the lives of these students. They may not remember the Sunday school series from last year, but there's a good chance that the truths they learned during a difficult time will be rooted deeply in their hearts.

Also, if we expect students to be honest with us, we should be willing to do the same with them. Sometimes students need you to step back from the curriculum so that you can testify about how God is moving in your life. Methodology isn't the most important thing. Rather, living what you preach is the most effective way to teach.

- **John Sinkhorn,** Student Pastor, Immanuel Free Will Baptist Church, Winterville, North Carolina

---

HOPE IN THE WORD

Looking at the monumental task of teaching the Bible properly to teenagers can cause us to feel inadequate. And as we consider the challenges and burdens of ministry, we can easily become discouraged. Yet we can find hope within the pages of Scripture.

Thinking back again to Ezekiel 37, we see that God commands him to speak to a valley of dry bones. Ezekiel is faithful, doing what the LORD commands, and he sees the transformation that God's Word has on these bones. Flesh begins to come upon them, and life enters into them.

Only through the proclaiming, sharing, and living of God's Word can we accomplish anything for the Kingdom of Christ. Only through the proclamation of God's Word, applied by God's Spirit, can the church grow and flourish.

As the Father, Spirit, and Son were at work within the creation of the universe, they are also at work within the creation and transformation of each believer.

Ultimately, preaching and teaching God's Word is not about our ability. Rather, we rest and trust in the empowered work of the Holy Spirit. As Hebrews 4:12 states, "The word of God is living and active, sharper than any two-edged sword, piercing to the division of soul and of spirit, of joints and of marrow, and discerning the thoughts and intentions of the heart."

Remember this: God's Word is living—and it's powerful. It's God, working through His Word and Spirit, who is transforming your students into the likeness of Christ. In the end, your faithfulness to Scripture is the most important consideration. Remember, you don't accomplish this transformative work; God through you does. Hope in God's Word, and it will transform your ministry and your students.

Discussion Questions

1. How do we find the meaning of a passage?
2. What imbalance can easily lead to poor teaching?
3. How do we keep our teaching and preaching Christ-centered?
4. What three worlds must the youth pastor understand to teach teenagers properly?
5. How does hoping in God's Word change our teaching?
6. In what ways in which we can we "build a bridge"?

Helpful Resources

Doug Fields and Duffy Robbins, *Speaking to Teenagers: How to Think About, Create, and Deliver Effective Messages* (El Cajon, Calif.: Youth Specialties, 2007).

Jonathan Leeman, *Reverberation: How God's Word Brings Light, Freedom, and Action to His People* (Wheaton, Ill.: Moody, 2011).

Walt Mueller, *Engaging the Soul of Youth Culture: Bridging Teen Worldviews and Christian Truth* (Downers Grove, Ill.: InterVarsity, 2006).

Lawrence O. Richards and Gary J. Bredfelt, *Creative Bible Teaching* (Chicago: Moody, 1998).

John Stott, *Between Two Worlds: The Challenge of Preaching Today* (Grand Rapids, Mich.: Eerdmans, 1982).

CHAPTER 10

MINISTERING IN AN AGE OF DISTRACTION

"Technology always has unforeseen consequences, and it is not always clear, at the beginning, who or what will win, and who or what will lose."

- NEIL POSTMAN[1]

An image recently surfaced on Twitter showing the intense hold that electronic media has on children. The picture portrays a gathering of students in front of one of Rembrandt's most famous and moving pieces, *The Night Watch,* at Amsterdam's Rijksmuseum.[2]

Interesting yet unsurprising is the fact that none of the children are observing the painting; instead, all of them are looking at their phones. The opportunity to look at one of the greatest paintings of the last five hundred years, and they've opted for digital distraction (ironic).

No one, especially youth ministers and parents, needs to be told that contemporary technologies are having a profound effect on students (and adults) today. Too often youth ministers walk into a youth room to be greeted only by students' eyes glued to their screens. While the addiction may not surprise us, the long-term impact may.

Our culture is continuing to lead students deeper into their electronic escape. Youth ministers must think through how youth ministry itself has taken on the characteristics of a technology.[3] Therefore, my goal in this chapter is to help youth ministers think through the difficulties of ministering in this age of distraction and provide a hopeful way forward.

TECHNOLOGICAL TYRANNY

Technology has a stronghold on our students, these "digital natives."[4] If we're going to minister in this age of distraction, then we should analyze its possible hazards. Marva Dawn argues that the church's youth face six immediate dangers concerning media over-consumption: It (1) wastes so much time; (2) stifles the imagination; (3) causes children to develop smaller brains; (4) causes children to be less motivated to think; (5) promotes and fosters greed; and (6) muddles our perception of reality.[5]

While some of these dangers are intuitive, each of them poses challenges to the spiritual and mental health of children and students. We must think critically about how we should engage with digital technology within the church. I'm especially concerned with number six. The fact that media is not simply communicating information but also cultivating the way that youth understand the world should raise ministerial red flags.[6]

Our technological society is molded and ordered by the scenes we see on our electronic screens. We live in a time dominated by what Richard Weaver calls the "great stereopticon": the television. The television and other screens have become commonplace in our lives, and they hold sway over our understanding of the surrounding world.

Now that doesn't mean that everything we see on a television, computer, tablet, or smartphone is inherently bad (or good). It simply means that our culture is being changed by how it processes information.[7]

Youth ministry expert Walt Mueller writes, "In addition to shaping *what* they think, media is shaping *how* they think, and thereby distinguishing them even further from previous generations. Millennials are passive, easily bored, uneasy with quiet, often impatient and expectant of immediate gratification.... They are communicating, learning, perceiving and processing information in new and different ways."[8]

The technology that our students use on a regular basis is rewiring their minds. It's altering not only the content but also the means by which that content is received. This truth was recently illustrated by college students from different parts of the world who went twenty-four hours without any digital technology:

> From the United Kingdom: "Emptiness. Emptiness overwhelms me," "Unplugging . . . felt like turning off a life-support system," and, "I feel paralyzed."
>
> From China: "I sat in my bed and stared blankly. I had nothing to do," and, "The feeling of nothing passed into my heart. . . . I felt like I had lost something important."

> From Uganda: "I felt like there was a problem with me," "I counted down minute by minute and made sure I did not exceed even a single second more," and, "I felt so lonely."
>
> From the United States: "I went into absolute panic mode," and, "It felt as though I was being tortured."[9]

As you read these quotes, you're not sure whether to laugh or to cry. What is astounding is the similarity between these confessions and language used regarding substance abuse.[10]

These technologies are not simply neutral tools to be used for good or bad. Rather, they have intrinsic effects on those who utilize them. In some ways, as Nicholas Carr puts it, "a medium's content matters less than the medium itself in influencing how we think and act. . . . A popular medium molds what we see and how we see it."[11] The medium, combined with its message, by definition reorders how students understand the world in a powerful way.

Struggles with technology can come in a variety of ways. Media can reorient the way that a student thinks, but it can also weaken their mental capacities. Duke University professor Katherine Hayles states, "I can't get my students to read whole books anymore."[12] We've reached a significant milestone when a professor at a prestigious university can't convince her students to read an entire book.

Additionally, media use is increasing. According to a 2010 study by the Kaiser Family Foundation, media usage has increased to seven hours and thirty-eight minutes a day! That means that students are using media fifty hours a week. Greg Poppo from *USA Today* commented about this study, saying, "Kids these days spend so much time with electronic media—cellphones, iPods, video games and computers—that it might as well be a full-time job."[13]

Don't believe the statistics? Try an exercise that I use with my college students each year. Write on a board or on a handout various forms of media a given student might use (e.g., cell phone, laptop, mp3 player, radio, and/or television). Have the students write down how much time they spend on each kind of media per week.

If your results are anything like mine, you'll notice that most students can give a general number for most forms of technology: maybe four hours listening to the radio or fifteen hours on their laptop. However, when I ask students how much time they spend on their cell phones, they often can't give me an answer. They're unaware of the time that they spend away from the cell phone. For many of them, it's become as commonplace as their hands or their feet.

REMODELING TIP

Because "electronic technologies aren't going away anytime soon," it's crucial to establish a practical strategy for dealing with distracted students. Consider one negative and two positive suggestions:

DON'T fall into the technology trap yourself. Students don't need another Snapstreak. They need a shepherd. While you *should* educate yourself about every aspect of their culture, including technology, you don't have to be a social media maven to minister to them effectively. Understand that technology and social media can absorb time put to better use elsewhere.

DO make technology your friend. Rather than going on the attack, understand the fabric of student culture and *use* technology and media for illustrations, humorous examples, and discussion starters. And, while you don't want to appear to be hopelessly inept when it comes to technology, don't be afraid to poke fun at yourself when you aren't up on the latest trends and terminology.

DO take advantage of technology-free moments. It's a forty-six-hour round trip from Nashville, Tennessee, to Salt Lake City, Utah. I've made the round trip twice on summer mission trips.

A number of ministry friends have raised skeptical eyebrows, wondering if a four-hour flight wouldn't have been more effective. Absolutely not. My explanation is simple: For hundreds of miles across the American West, with limited cell coverage and monotonous scenery, I enjoyed uninterrupted conversation with my students—no distractions. I let them guide the discussion, from how to know the will of God to finding the right husband/wife and everything in between.

Today, a number of those same students are actively involved in ministry and point to those conversations as life altering. When establishing your youth group calendar, make strategic choices to create technology-free, distraction-free moments that allow you to speak into the lives of your students.

- **Eric Thomsen,** Managing Editor, *ONE Magazine*, National Association of Free Will Baptists, Antioch, Tennessee

---

CHRONOLOGICAL SNOBBERY

In a sense, technology can reinforce a desire for the new. Gregg Moder, a scholar and a father, writes, "Ultimately, the technological sentiments of our offspring reflect a specific narrative (belief system) that is deeply embedded within western culture."[14] Moder is right when he argues that an incessant focus on technology reinforces an idolatry of progress.

Every time I turn around, it seems, there's a new phone, new gadget, or new app about which my teenagers are conversing. I reveal my magnitude of un-coolness when I inquire about new fads (if that's what they even call them anymore).

With few exceptions, the majority of products we use are marketed as "new and improved." Our computers, telephones, and tablets need constant updates to stay current. Wait too long and the razor you use or the clothes you wear will be archaic, or worse yet, passé. We live in a world that's hooked on the "now." We want what's new, hip, and current—especially if we can get it before anyone else.

Unfortunately, this occurs almost always at the expense of the past. Therefore, we must do some personal triage and diagnose whether we're guilty of "chronological snobbery." To begin, we should understand the problem, and then we can consider a treatment.

C. S. Lewis, who coined the term *chronological snobbery*, struggled (ironically) with the relevance of Christianity. Before his conversion, he couldn't see how a nearly two-thousand-year-old religion could have relevance to his time. Thankfully, his friend Owen Barfield helped him understand that the antiquity of Christianity was the exact reason it was relevant in his day (and in our day, as well). Specifically, because Christianity transcends time, it's not under the bondage of any era, Barfield explained. After coming to this realization, this became a main tenet in Lewis's philosophy which would saturate his writings.

Lewis defined chronological snobbery as "the uncritical acceptance of the intellectual climate common to our own age and the assumption that whatever has gone out of date is on that account discredited." Explaining the problems of this mindset, he continued, "You must find out why it went out of date. Was it ever refuted (and if so by whom, where, and how conclusively) or did it merely die away as fashions do? If the latter, this tells us nothing about its truth or falsehood."[15]

"From seeing this," he explained further, "one passes to the realization that our own age is also 'a period,' and certainly has, like all periods, its own characteristic illusions. They are likeliest to lurk in those widespread assumptions which are so ingrained in the age that no one dares to attack or feels it necessary to defend them."[16]

Simply put, chronological snobbery is the perception that all things new are good and that all things old are bad. The only qualifier given to ideas, people, and objects is whether they're current. Whether something is true, noble, or simply good is irrelevant; only the fact that it's contemporary matters. This haughty snobbishness throws the baby out with the bath water and replaces the tub.

Some may wonder whether chronological snobbery is really all that bad. Should we really worry about the past if we've already figured everything out in the present? That's the problem: We don't know everything. If we focus only on the present, dire consequences will follow.

"It is not the remembered but the forgotten past that enslaves us. I think the same is true of society," explained Lewis in his inaugural lectures at Cambridge University. "To study the past does indeed liberate us from the present, from the idols of our own market-place. But I think it liberates us from the past too. I think no class of men are less enslaved to the past than historians. The unhistorical are usually, without knowing it, enslaved to a fairly recent past."[17]

Cliché though it may sound, those who forget about the past are doomed to repeat it. Knowledge of the past not only liberates us from our own era's snobbery; it also liberates us from the snobberies of other eras. If we keep our eyes focused on the now, we'll lose sight of the rich treasures of the past. Such amnesia keeps us under the bondage of both the today and the yesterday, and it will always come up empty-handed.

Case in point: If we interact with only the contemporary, we'll miss the great tradition of Christian hymns, books, and preachers. We'll forget about Isaac Watts's melodic "Alas, and Did My Savior Bleed," John Owen's sobering *The Mortification of Sin*, and John Chrysostom's beautiful homilies.

Though our students may not enjoy some of these older classics, they're vital. They're some of the foundations on which our theology is developed and through which God has worked. When we're stuck in the now, we have nothing to build on. We become like trees with no roots, buildings with no foundations. It's not just a bad perspective; it's a losing one.

By critiquing chronological snobbery, we're not saying that new things are never good. The point is that when we accept them uncritically, the outcome can be dangerous. Some new things are terrific, but newness doesn't spell greatness. Actually quite the contrary: Because time hasn't tested new things through decades, or even centuries or millennia, of scrutiny, they can't hold the same weight as those older things that still remain. Moder expounds further:

> This is reminiscent of Genesis 11 and the Tower of Babel. Today it seems we are at the cusp of another

> such moment in history. Bricks and mortar are amassing. The world is troubled, yet abuzz with anticipation of what might exist just beyond the next technological threshold. The story of technological progress has become in some people's minds an end in itself. This is a wild grasp beyond the biblical narrative and in the opposite direction. Our [teens] will need theological guidance and support in the future because those who attempt to integrate their faith within their vocation, in a number of fields, will potentially face significant challenges. . . . This impending challenge presents a call to build a theological foundation for a practical theology of digital technological use. It is a call to remember amongst ourselves and to teach our children that digital technology, and our use of it, is in our hearts and "in our heads, not just in our hands."[18]

ONE (MORE) REAL PROBLEM

Maybe this last problem will help us to connect the dots. Recently, during our Wednesday night study, we watched a video presentation. It included an illustration that really got our students talking.[19] Halfway through the lesson, the host asked us to imagine a room full of screens. In this imaginary room, ceiling to floor, crammed in every nook and cranny possible, are screens and monitors projecting events from your life. Everything you've ever done is open for all to see in this room.

Some episodes you'd want recorded and played for

every friend you have. However, this room doesn't broadcast only the good stuff; it also shows the bad stuff. These monitors reveal every text message you've ever sent, every website you've ever visited, and every sin you've ever committed when you thought no one else was around. As you can imagine, none of these students were excited about the prospect of this room. They'd be ashamed, embarrassed, and distraught if their entire lives were on display for all to see.

Note the irony: These same students, who banished the idea of such technological sophistication putting their life on display, nonetheless embraced screens, gadgets, and social media in order to feel connected. They put their thoughts, emotions, and heartbreak onto social media for the world to see, but they don't realize the vulnerability that this exposes since they don't experience the immediate discomfort of receiving disapproving looks and gentle rebukes. Social media and other technologies permit students to "be themselves" with an apparent low risk of vulnerability.

My wife has often described social media as an adult's imaginary friend. We tweet and update everything that we'd want to tell someone who we knew would never disapprove. These are often the comments and declarations that we'd never say person-to-person. In fact, social media is an imaginary buffer between our emotions and reality.

At the heart of the issue are students who want to be loved deeply. Scripture testifies, like the imaginary room discussed above, that nothing can be hidden from God. We cannot hide in secret places from Him (Jeremiah 23:24) or disguise the secrets of our hearts (Psalm 44:21). Hebrews 4:13 tells us clearly, "No creature is hidden from His sight, but all are naked and exposed to the eyes of Him to whom we must give account."

While our screen-filled room may not exist, the omnipresent eyes of God do. He sees us for who we really are: sinful, wreaked, hurting people. And although teenagers often run to social media to feel connected and accepted, something far better is available to them.

REMODELING TIP

One of the ways our church has implemented the concepts discussed in this chapter is by creating multigenerational ministries. For example, before Wednesday night Bible studies, everyone gathers in one building for music and prayer before going to their separate classes. This enables the youth to rub shoulders with the older saints in our church.

We also have "Titus 2 events" that are specifically designed to mingle the different generations. These events aren't overtly entertaining, and yet they're some of our most popularly attended. This flies in the face of the conventional wisdom that suggests that teens are interested only in events that are fun.

The fruit of these events is most vividly displayed when one of our senior saints goes to the nursing home or else to be with the Lord. We often fill two vans to the brim with mostly youth who ride three hours just to visit one of our ladies in an assisted living center. At funerals, I've seen the eyes of numerous juniors and teens dripping with tears for the loss of an older saint with whom they shared no familial relation.

They travel and they weep, because they've formed intensely meaningful relationships with these older members. They've heard repeatedly the stories our elders share of the sufficiency of their walk with the Lord to get them through the darkest times of life. In light of such stories, the latest fads lose their glimmer.

As youth leaders, do we believe that youth want only entertainment? Or do stories such as these not suggest that students find fulfillment through the ordinary means of grace, through fellowshipping with the body through prayer and song and Bible intake?

- **Derek Cominskie,** Youth Pastor, Tippett's Chapel Free Will Baptist Church, Clayton, North Carolina

---

RECALIBRATING DESIRE

"What is the solution?" we might ask. Upon seeing that youth ministry itself has roots in this technological age, how do we minister in light of this legacy, and how do we minister to students who are inundated in it? The answer lies in leading students to recalibrating their desires.

At Welch College, where I teach, our senior history professor shares a story with which others can sympathize: His children, throughout their childhood, always drank orange juice from concentrate. For the uninitiated, juice from concentrate is an icy mush from a paper and tin can that you mix in water to make a pitcher of juice. While concentrate is inexpensive, its quality leaves something to be longed for.

One day, though, for a special occasion, he bought the best juice that money could buy. We can all imagine: wonderful, hand-squeezed, authentic Florida orange juice. Our mouths water at the sound. But the youngsters were surprised. In his own words: "I picked up the new freshly squeezed orange juice, though we'd been accustomed to the concentrate. In response, my son asked what was wrong with the orange juice. My son was like many of us are. We become accustomed to the cheap for so long that, when we taste the good, the good tastes odd." The flavorful juice before him, this professor's son wanted the metallic-tasting, mushy concentrate.[20]

Such is the struggle for youth pastors (and all pastors). In many ways, we're trying to renew and reorient the desires of youth. For so long, they've been submerged in the distraction-laden world of social media and electronic screens. All that these technologies can offer are passing moments of temporary gratification.

Our goal in ministry isn't for students to desire less but more. We don't want them to settle for fickle, passing pleasures but to long for the joy of eternity that exists in God alone. Lewis remarked, "We are half-hearted creatures, fooling about with drink and sex and ambition when infinite joy is offered us, like an ignorant child who wants to go on making mud pies in a slum because he cannot imagine what is meant by the offer of a holiday at the sea. We are far too easily pleased."[21]

How do we renew or transform desires? How do we, in practical ways, help students see that what the gospel and Scripture offer are much grander than anything that this world can offer? The answer is that we should point our students to the transcendence of God. We should give them a taste of the vertical spectrum and teach them to savor the depth of truth and the height of glory.

First, we must encourage students to give roots to their faith. This comes through the formulation of a biblical worldview. This will help change not only *what* students think but also *how* they think. Youth workers must equip students with the resources to think through theological problems, ethical situations, and philosophical questions. This results from biblical instruction that touches on every facet of life. It can be accomplished only by leading students deep into their faith and allowing them to root themselves in Christ (Colossians 2:7).

Second, we must lead students to long for something greater and more wonderful than anything else in the world can offer them, including electronic media. We must help them to desire the object of glory.

C. S. Lewis called this our *sehnsucht*, a German noun that's often translated as "yearning" or "longing." *Sehnsucht* implies a deep emotional state with this longing. Lewis wrote, "If I find in myself a desire which no experience in this world can satisfy, the most probable explanation is that I was made for another world."[22]

We lead students to this state by helping them taste glimpses of glory. This can come through any of the means of grace. The more that students experience biblical practices like deep scriptural intake, earnest prayer, meaningful fellowship, sacrificial service, the more they'll be dissatisfied with the temporary pleasures of this world's offerings. When they taste the foretastes of Christ's treasures practiced in the biblical community, man-made fads will no longer satisfy the yearnings of their hearts.

A BETTER WAY

In a way, Christ has seen this room full of screens. He's witnessed every terrible and shameful thing we've ever done, and still He loves us (Romans 5:8; 1 John 4:9-12) and offers us salvation (1 John 3:1). No form of media can ever demonstrate this for us.

From all indications, electronic technologies aren't going away anytime soon. But the more that youth pastors can give their students a taste of something greater, the less of a stranglehold that it will have on students. Take students deep. Show them the depth and wonders that our faith has for their lives today. At the same time, take students high, and show them the wonders and glories that are still to come.

Discussion Questions

1. How does technology affect student's perception of reality?
2. Out of the six dangers that Marva Dawn presents, which do you find more concerning? Why?
3. How does aiming to change our students' desires change our ministry practices?
4. In what ways does technology present a deeper spiritual problem in our students?
5. In what ways is chronological snobbery antithetical to the Christian faith? How do we see this in youth ministry?
6. What are some positive and negative ways that we can use digital technology in youth ministry?

Helpful Resources

Nicholas Carr, *The Shallows: What the Internet Is Doing to Our Brains* (New York: W. W. Norton, 2010).

Craig Detweiler, *iGods: How Technology Shapes Our Spiritual and Social Lives* (Grand Rapids, Mich.: Brazos, 2013).

Gregg Moder, "Approaching Wise Dialogue With Our Technological Test Pilots: Re-Framing the Story of Digital Progress," *The Journal of Youth Ministry*, vol. 15, no. 1 (Fall 2016).

Greg Poppo, "Kids' electronic media use jumps to 53 hours a week," *USA Today: Technology*, January 20, 2010; http://usatoday30.usatoday.com/tech/news/2010-01-20-1Avideokids20_ST_N.htm; accessed July 12, 2016; Internet.

Neil Postman, *Amusing Ourselves to Death: Public Discourse in the Age of Show Business* (New York: Penguin, 1985).

Andrew Zirschky, *Beyond the Screen: Youth Ministry for the Connected But Alone Generation* (Nashville: Abingdon, 2015).

CHAPTER 11

THE GOSPEL OF REST IN MINISTRY

"For you have made us for yourself and restless is our heart until it comes to rest in you."

- AUGUSTINE[1]

Most mornings I'm fortunate enough to be able to hit the snooze button once before diving headfirst into a day packed full of studying, responsibilities, and tasks. I'll always drink a few cups of coffee throughout the day to keep myself alert and moving forward. I check off my to-dos as I prepare for my college courses, review Sunday school curriculum, and plan activities.

Upon arriving home, I finish my honey-do list, work on some coursework or an article, and take care of our dog. On a good day, I even indulge in an episode of *Doctor Who* or *Sherlock* before going to bed and starting all over again. Like Greek mythology's Sisyphus, I push the proverbial boulder up the hill, just to watch it roll back down for me to repeat the process.

I'm not alone. Busyness is an equal opportunity employer. Working hard isn't exclusive to pastors, or even

Christians for that matter. We work hard, and rightly so (1 Corinthians 10:31; Colossians 3:17). We hope and pray that our diligent work and faithful obedience bring glory to God. Important imperatives call us to committed service.

Unfortunately, busyness often comes to the detriment of our rest. Parents sometimes tell me that their child will be at youth group after ball practice, but only if they finish their piano lessons and homework first. Our initial reaction is to get angry. We justify that we are equally as busy; we make church a priority, so why can't they? Before we know it, we have also turned the things of God into a checklist of to-dos.

Living in this time-is-money society, how do we teach our students about rest? Is it just a license for laziness? Or is it something that's found at the heart of the gospel? The Bible talks extensively about rest (Exodus 33:14; Isaiah 30:15; Psalm 127:2).

But what does the Bible say about *how* we should rest? Are we to work more or rest more? A cursory view of any concordance shows ample mentions of "rest" and "sleep." From the imperatives in the Ten Commandments of the Sabbath to the resting of the saints in Revelation, the Bible holds a thread of rest from beginning to end. Essentially, Scripture teaches three truths about the gospel and the rest it proclaims.

REST: PAST, PRESENT, AND FUTURE

In the second book of the Bible, God ordains one day a week for us not to work but to rest (Exodus 20:8-11). This is the Lord's Day; it's the Sabbath. In Genesis 2, God Himself gives us this example. After creating the world in six days, He rested on the seventh.

Ponder this amazing truth: God's seventh day was mankind's first. God first worked six days and then rested. Adam's and Eve's first day was a day of rest. In a sense, mankind was created for Sabbath. God made us to rest in His sufficiency. By no means is work a result of the fall, though; Adam and Eve stewarded the Garden of Eden. The wariness we experience from work, however, is a result of sin.

The phenomenon of rest isn't simply a thing of the past; it's a thing of the present and of the future. It's not just a historical asterisk. The Bible tells us that rest is available for us in Christ today. There is a present component of rest. Jesus says, "Come to me, all who labor and are heavy laden, and I will give you rest. Take my yoke upon you, and learn from me, for I am gentle and lowly in heart, and you will find rest for your souls. For my yoke is easy, and my burden is light" (Matthew 11:28-29).

Christ releases us from our earthly burdens; He alone offers rest for our weary souls. While this rest isn't yet fully realized, as it will be in the new heavens and new earth, we can nonetheless rest in it today. He gives us peace in troubled circumstances, hope in a broken world, and assurance that the hardships of this world are but a vapor.

When the labors of this life are too heavy, always remember that Christ gives a profound invitation. One day the rest of those whose hope is in Christ will be perfect. The future offers comforting prospects. The New Testament describes believers who've died as "sleeping" (John 11:11-14; 1 Thessalonians 5:9-11; 1 Corinthians 15:20).

This privilege is extended only to the heirs of Christ, though. Hebrews 4:1-2 explains, "Therefore, while the promise of entering his rest still stands, let us fear lest any of you should seem to have failed to reach it. For good news came to us just as to them, but the message they heard did not benefit them, because they were not united by faith with those who listened."

We are promised the fullness of God's rest only if we're redeemed in Christ. Nowhere does Scripture suggest that the unredeemed will be given this blessing. Believers don't die in an ultimate sense. Rather, they're awaiting their glorious resurrection bodies.

REDEMPTION AND REST

While we've considered its implications from the past and for the future, how does the scriptural truth of rest change the way that we live our lives and guide our ministries from day to day? The early church father Augustine helps us with this question.

Restless Until Christ

In *Confessions*, Augustine famously began his autobiography, "For you have made us for yourself and restless is our heart until it comes to rest in you."[2] Augustine contrasted our pre-redemptive states of restlessness from our post-redemptive states of joy and peace that comes only by faith in Christ.

Before we put our trust in Christ, we're restless, for the magnitude of sin weighs heavy upon our souls. We're at enmity with our Creator, and an eternal gap divides Him from us. However, faith in the gospel of Jesus Christ reconciles us to God, giving us rest for our souls. Rest, then, is found in redemption.

If we're fully to realize this rest, we must have a full understanding of the gospel:

> The one and only God, who is holy, made us in his image to know him (Gen. 1:26-28). But we sinned and cut ourselves off from him (Gen. 3; Rom. 3:23). In his great love, God sent his Son Jesus to come as king and rescue his people from their enemies—most significantly their own sin (Ps. 2; Luke 1:67-79). Jesus established his kingdom by acting as both a mediating priest and a priestly sacrifice—he live a perfect life and died on the cross, thus fulfilling the law himself and taking on himself the punishment for the sins of many (Mark 10:45; John 1:14; Heb. 7:26; Rom. 3:21-26, 5:12-21); then he rose again from the dead, showing that God accepted his sacrifice and that God's wrath against us had been exhausted (Acts 2:24, Rom. 4:25). He now calls us to repent of our sins and trust in Christ alone for our forgiveness (Acts 17:30, John 1:12). If we repent of our sins and trust in Christ, we are born again into a new life, an eternal life with God (John 3:16).[3]

Shouldn't a book on youth ministry have begun with a definition of the gospel? My reason for waiting until now is twofold. First, as you near the end of this book (and may forget everything else you've read—I hope not!), I want you to remember the gospel. This book is a vapor in the wind (James 4:14) compared to the eternal good news of Jesus Christ. The gospel is the center, the heart, and the reason we do everything we do. Without it, we are clanging symbols and resounding brass (1 Corinthians 13:1).

Second, the gospel is necessary as we continue in ministry. Yes, the gospel is the way we become Christians. But it's also necessary to remain in the faith. We need its glorious truth every minute of every day. As Lamentations 3:22-23 explains, "The steadfast love of the LORD never ceases; his mercies never come to an end; they are new every morning; great is your faithfulness."

At the heart of the gospel is this beautiful good news: you are justified in Christ. When God looks at you, He doesn't see your terrible sins and depraved thoughts. Instead, He sees Christ's righteousness. Paul tells us, "For our sake he made him to be sin who knew no sin, so that in him we might become the righteousness of God." (2 Corinthians 5:21). The familiar passage of Ephesians 2:1-10 boasts:

> And you were dead in the trespasses and sins in which you once walked, following the course of this world, following the prince of the power of the air, the spirit that is now at work in the sons of disobedience—among whom we all once lived in the passions of our flesh, carrying out the desires of the body and the mind, and were by nature children of wrath, like the rest of mankind. But God, being rich in mercy,

> because of the great love with which he loved us, even when we were dead in our trespasses, made us alive together with Christ—by grace you have been saved—and raised us up with him and seated us with him in the heavenly places in Christ Jesus, so that in the coming ages he might show the immeasurable riches of his grace in kindness toward us in Christ Jesus. *For by grace you have been saved through faith. And this is not your own doing; it is the gift of God, not a result of works, so that no one may boast. For we are his workmanship, created in Christ Jesus for good works, which God prepared beforehand, that we should walk in them.*[4]

My brother or sister in Christ, your justification before God isn't, in any way, achieved by your works. Your good works of the law will never be good enough (Isaiah 64:6). Instead, your justification is achieved according to the saving work of Christ alone (Romans 3:28; 4:5; 5:1; 11:6; Galatians 2:16, 21). The gospel isn't good news only at the beginning of your Christian life; it's good news everyday of your Christian life, which directs and transforms the way you live life and pursue ministry.

We can rest in ministry because we know that our works don't save us. No matter how many calls I make, activities I schedule, or lessons I teach, none of them save my soul; they are but a response of gratitude to the one who did. Indeed, the gospel is the greatest news in universe. It reminds us that our ministries aren't about us, and they don't depend on us.

An Otherworldly Rest

The doctrine of rest changes our lives and our ministries in a second way. Augustine wrote, "I have read in Plato and Cicero sayings that are wise and very beautiful; but I have never read in either of them: Come unto me all ye that labor and are heavy laden."[5]

The rest that Christ offers us is something of which the world knows not. That Christ, God incarnate, has borne all of life's burdens for us is a gift beyond our wildest imaginations. Not only has Jesus endured the payment of our sin, but He's also offered us a rest in Him that the world can't fully comprehend. Christ offers both redemption for our souls and release from the weight of the world.

Does divine rest give believers license to be lazy? As the apostle Paul might say, "By no means!" Hebrews 4:9-10 says, "So then, there remains a Sabbath rest for the people of God, for whoever has entered God's rest has also rested from his works as God did from his." Our rest is both already and not yet. We rest in Christ now, and we will also rest in Him fully for all eternity.

"The writer of Hebrews speaks of a promised Sabbath rest that is a rest of salvation—both present experience and eschatological expectation," explains Albert Mohler about Hebrews 4:9-10. "This rest is accomplished by the atonement of the Lord Jesus Christ, perfectly accomplished for us as He paid in full the penalty of our sins. Thus, the most important issue of Sabbath rest in the New Testament is that we rest in Christ and we rest from our labors—from all efforts to be saved by our works."[6]

Mohler says it wonderfully. As a Christian, all rest finds its center and purpose in the work and person of Jesus Christ. Our rest, just like our ministries, is fixed on Jesus Christ our Lord.

GIVING GOD GLORY

Scripture points us to rest in a rest that Christ alone offers. How do we do this if man's "chief end" is "to glorify God"?[7] Don't we need to do something give Him the praise due His name?

By resting, we admit that we aren't God; only God is God. The fact that our bodies need rest is a testament to our finitude and mortality. Only God, who's omnipotent and sovereign, can perpetually create and work without rest. It's only for our benefit and instruction that He rested in the beginning. By resting, we show through our actions that only God is God. Isaiah 40:28-31 reads:

> Have you not known? Have you not heard? The Lord is the everlasting God, the Creator of the ends of the earth. He does not faint or grow weary; his understanding is unsearchable. He gives power to the faint, and to him who has no might he increases strength. Even youths shall faint and be weary, and young men shall fall exhausted; but they who wait for the Lord shall renew their strength; they shall mount up with wings like eagles; they shall run and not be weary; they shall walk and not faint.

By finding our rest in Christ, we also admit that we, with our merits, are unable to accomplish salvation.

As Christians, we have an opportunity that's not available to those outside of Christ's covenant community. Because we're found in Christ, we don't have to worry about validating our existence; we depend wholly on the work of Jesus. Because of that, we can rest: in our redemption, in the peace He gives, and in death.

The next time you find yourself in the heap of a busy schedule or frustrated at your students for theirs, remember that we live our lives in light of a gospel of rest. We don't serve a God who's adding to our burdens, but one who's removing the heaviness of our yokes. We don't herald more to-dos but rather the great and glorious "it is finished" (John 19:30). Because of that, we can rest in Christ alone.

REMODELING TIP

If I don't plan to rest, I don't rest. As an ambitious, over-achieving, seminarian, dad, husband, blogger, and Crossfitter, my default is to sleep less and to do more. By His grace, God has surrounded me with people who tell me that, sometimes, I need to make time to go home, date my wife, and simply rest.

Those voices remind me that I'm not God. If I'm going to be a better husband and dad, then I might not deliver as good a sermon or get as good a grade on that paper. Being surrounded with people and pastors committed to my rest and my enjoyment of that rest should be a first priority. These, after all, are the men that remind me to rest.

Practically, what should rest look like in the chaos of student ministry? First, set a time to be home each day. Because my schedule is crazy and I don't always know when I'll get to work, I count eight hours from whenever I start working. I tell my wife that time, and she keeps me accountable. Second, make hourly goals in the morning. The most important go first. If I have more tasks than I can complete in eight hours, then I cut something.

If I finish early, I go home. Third, take Friday and Saturday off, not visiting students or even doing yard work. Don't work on anything.

Fourth, plan two or three "days of solitude" each year. I go to a neighboring city or tour my favorite coffee shops. Whatever it is, spend the day alone, reading, praying, and thinking. My boss counts this as a workday, leaving my vacation time untouched. Fifth, schedule two brief vacations before and after the craziness of summer to spend with your family. For example, whenever I return from camp or a mission trip, I take a day or two off in the next work week and have someone preach the next time I'm scheduled.

- **Seth Stewart,** Pastor of Student Ministries, Bridgeway Church, Oklahoma City, Oklahoma

---

Discussion Questions

1. How is Christian rest already but not yet?
2. In what ways is there a past, present, and future component to the way Christians rest?
3. How is rest connected to the gospel?
4. What does your justification in Christ mean for the way you do ministry?
5. How does rest give glory to God?
6. What are tangible ways in which you can practice the principles of this chapter?

Helpful Resources

Audrey Barrick, "Youth Ministries Teaching Behavior Modification, Not the Gospel?" *The Christian Post: Church and Ministries*, April 17, 2012; http://www.christianpost.com/news/youth-ministries-teaching-behavior-modification not-gospel-73408/; accessed October 11, 2016; Internet.

Cameron Cole, "Busy All the Time: Over-Scheduled Children and the Freedom of the Gospel," *The Gospel Coalition,*

January 12, 2014; https://www.thegospelcoalition.org/article/busy-all-the-time/; accessed November 10, 2016; Internet.

R. Kent and Barbara Hughes, *Liberating Ministry from the Success Syndrome* (Wheaton, Ill.: Crossway, 2008).

Paul David Tripp, *Dangerous Calling: Confronting the Unique Challenges of Pastoral Ministry* (Wheaton, Ill.: Crossway, 2012).

CONCLUSION

"You are chief theologian and biblical interpreter for the young people who gather around you."

- ANDREW ZIRCHSKY[I]

I began this book with one request: that you think more deeply about your work in youth ministry. While we certainly haven't covered everything that youth ministry includes, we've walked together through some deeper elements of youth ministry.

We've asked hard questions about the foundations and future of youth ministry, as well as some needed changes. We've talked about everything from purpose to apologetics to teaching to sustainable change. We've even considered a way forward for modern-day youth ministry. We've covered much ground in a few short pages.

The difference that this book can make depends on how you respond. As with any book, you might simply place it on your shelf, where it will collect dust and forget about it. Or you can allow it to penetrate the way you think about ministry. You can put the prescriptions of this book into practice.

Really, I want this book, and ultimately everything that you do in youth ministry, to result in more than just deeper thinking. That's not enough. My hope is that God uses this book to challenge the work of your head, heart, and hands.

My hope is that this book not only challenges your thinking but also helps you to have a deeper heart for your students and a stronger resolve to do something about it.

DON'T STOP

Additionally, don't stop with this book, and don't stop with the next. Continue to learn. Continue to grow and dive more deeply in your own faith and ministry. That's how you'll reach the next generation of believers. Get these resources and digest them.

Read books with which you agree and those with which you don't. Chew on those things that cause you to pause; spit out the stuff that's useless. Sharpen your mind as you flesh out your understanding of youth ministry. The worst thing you can do for yourself or for your students is to be complacent in ministry.

Second, don't trek this journey alone. Even outside this book, consider youth ministry with your volunteers, other youth pastors, and your pastor. Discuss your ideas. Talk about how you can connect your theology to your practice.

Also, if you've not already done so, find a good mentor who's more mature in the faith; fewer things in the Christian life are more beneficial. By spending time with a mentor, you can see and hear biblical ministry lived out. Make sure that individual is someone you deeply respect in Christian leadership. If you don't understand something, ask your mentor those hard questions.

Youth leader, you play an integral role in the lives of your students. Your work and dedication isn't wasted. It's difficult and dirty work. It is often thankless. You work much more than people realize: You're receiving those late-night calls from a student who just needs to talk. You're at the coffee shop taking students deeper into the Bible. You're caring for your own heart as you seek Christlikeness.

As you toil every day, studying Scripture and caring for teenagers, you're making a difference. You're contributing to the work of the Kingdom! There isn't any more important work than this. Ultimately, it's not you, but Christ in you (Galatians 2:20). Glory be to God that He uses such people as you and me, otherwise altogether unworthy, to accomplish His transformational work.

HOPE IN GOD

My prayer is that this book has helped you think about how your ministry can better reflect the principles and instructions in Scripture. Of course, there's more to be mined in the Bible. Spend time daily seeking His face. There's nothing we can do apart from God's revelation to us in the Bible. We're lost without His truth. May we always allow Him to guide our steps and light our paths (Psalm 119:105).

As you do all that you can for your youth ministry, remember that God is doing something amazing through you. When you come to the end of your abilities and strength—and you will—don't lose heart. God has indwelled you with His Spirit, giving you strength that isn't yours. He's entrusted us with the message of reconciliation from our all-sufficient Savior.

The truth that God empowers us is a magnificent honor

and responsibility. As we turn back to biblical models to grow youth in Christ, not only will students enjoy them, but they will be transformed by them.

We will observe God doing a work in our students that we clearly know is far beyond anything we can do on our own. We will see addictions broken, identities restored, relationships reconciled, and teenagers committing their lives and eternities to Christ our Lord. This, my friends, is the greatest privilege we could receive!

I want to leave you with this: Hope in God. Romans 15:13 says, "May the God of hope fill you with all joy and peace in believing, so that by the power of the Holy Spirit you may abound in hope." My friend, in all things, especially in your ministry, hope in God. Trust in Him to accomplish His good work.

When you're exhausted from activities and days of work, rest in God. When you're unsure if you're making a difference in the lives of students, trust in God. When you're filled with doubt, believe in God. Outside of Him, we can do nothing. Trust in His ways. For in this, we give God glory and honor and praise!

NOTES

Introduction

1 J. C. Ryle, *Thoughts for Young Men* (Carlisle, Penn.: The Banner of Truth Trust, 2016), 9; the language in this quotation has been modernized.

2 Warren S. Benson, "A Theology of Youth Ministry," in *The Complete Book of Youth Ministry*, eds. Warren S. Benson and Mark H. Senter III (Chicago: Moody, 1987), 17-18.

3 Dean Borgman, *Foundations for Youth Ministry: Theological Engagement with Teen Life and Culture* (Grand Rapids, Mich.: Baker Academic, 2013), ix.

4 Ryle, 28.

5 *A Treatise of the Faith and Practices of the National Association of Free Will Baptists* (Nashville: Executive Office, National Association of Free Will Baptists, 2008), 3.

Chapter 1

1 Andrew Root and Kenda Creasy Dean, *The Theological Turn in Youth Ministry* (Downers Grove, Ill.: Intervarsity, 2011), 20.

2 Concerning the development of youth ministry in America, see Thomas E. Bergler, *The Juvenilization of American Christianity* (Grand Rapids, Mich.: Eerdmans, 2012). Bergler traces four church movements over the past century and their efforts to minister to the next generation. Also, see Mark Senter, *When God Shows Up: A History of Protestant Youth Ministry in America* (Grand Rapids, Mich.: Baker Academic, 2010).

3 Abby Carr, "Youth Groups Driving Christian Teens to Abandon Faith" *Charisma News*, October 22, 2013; http://www.charismanews.com/us/41465-youth-groups-driving-christian-teens-to-abandon-faith; accessed July 15, 2016; Internet. Ed Stetzer has noted the terrible quality of this research. It was facilitated by the Center itself, consisted of only three questions and rewarded surveyors with a book (against youth ministry) upon completion of the survey. See Ed Stetzer, "Are Youth Groups Bad? A Rant on Bad Research," *Christianity Today*, May 19, 2014, http://www.christianitytoday.com/edstetzer/2014/may/are-youth-groups-bad.html; accessed July 15, 2016; Internet.

4 *A Treatise of the Faith and Practices of the National Association of Free Will Baptists* (Nashville: Executive Office, National Association of Free Will Baptists, 2008), 3.

5 Alvin L. Reid, *As You Go: Creating a Missional Culture of Gospel-Centered Students* (Colorado Springs: NavPress, 2013), 89.

6 By *confessional*, I'm referring to believers that hold to the orthodox, biblical beliefs of the church as articulated in the historic creeds and confessions of the faith. By *communal*, I'm referring to the church gathered for worship, the members of which live life accountable to one another as a unified Christian community.

7 Gregg Allison argues the church possesses the seven following attributes: (1) doxological, (2) logocentric, (3) pneuma-dynamic, (4) covenantal, (5) confessional, (6) missional, and (7) eschatological. See Gregg R. Allison, *Sojourners and Strangers: The Doctrine of the Church*, Foundations of Evangelical Theology, gen. ed. John S. Feinberg (Wheaton, Ill.: Crossway, 2012), 29.

8 *Sehnsucht* is a German noun that is often translated as meaning "yearning" or "longing." However, we don't have a perfect English equivalent because *Sehnsucht* implies a deep emotional state with this longing. This became a very popular theme in many of C. S. Lewis's writings. See C. S. Lewis, *Christian Reflections* (Grand Rapids, Mich.: Eerdmans, 2014); C. S. Lewis, *Surprised by Joy: The Shape of My Early Life* (San Diego: Harcourt, Brace, Jovanovich, 1966); and C. S. Lewis, "The Weight of Glory," in *The Weight of Glory and other Essays* (Grand Rapids, Mich.: Eerdmans, 1965). *Sehnsucht* is also a consistent theme in Marva Dawn's work. See Marva J. Dawn, *Is It A Lost Cause? Having the Heart of God for the Church's Children* (Grand Rapids, Mich.: Eerdmans, 1997).

9 Kenda Creasy Dean, *Almost Christian: What the Faith of Our Teenagers is Telling the American Church* (New York: Oxford University Press, 2010), 83. This book explores the findings of the National Study of Youth and Religion, completed by Christian Smith and Lisa Pearce. You can find the complete study at *National Study of Youth and Religion*; http://youthandreligion.nd.edu; accessed July 15, 2016; Internet.

10 See Paul G. Kelly, "A Theology of Youth," *Journal for Baptist Theology and Ministry*, vol. 13, no. 1 (Spring 2016): 17.

11 Ibid.

12 See Scottie May, et al., *Children Matter: Celebrating Their Place in the Church, Family, and Community* (Grand Rapids, Mich.: Eerdmans, 2005), 165-66.

13 Mike Kipp, "Is 'Youth Ministry' in the Bible? Researching the Scripture Behind Youth and Family Ministry," *Fuller Youth Institute*, July 30, 2012; http://fulleryouthinstitute.org/articles/is-youth-ministry-in-the-bible; accessed January 9, 2015; Internet.

14 Ibid.

15 Dave Keehn, "Biblical Mandate for Youth Ministry (Part 3): Youth Ministry in the New Testament," *The Good Book Blog*, March 5, 2012; http://www.thegoodbookblog.com/2012/mar/05/biblical-mandate-for-youth-ministry-part-3-youth-m/; accessed January 9, 2015; Internet.

16 Reid, 86.

Chapter 2

1 Mark DeVries, *Sustainable Youth Ministry: Why Most Youth Ministry Doesn't Last and What Your Church Can Do About It* (Downers Grove, Ill.: InterVarsity, 2008), 19.

2 See Mark H. Senter III, "Basic Models of Youth Ministry," in *Reaching a Generation for Christ: A Comprehensive Guide to Youth Ministry*, eds. Richard R. Dunn and Mark H. Senter III (Chicago: Moody, 1997); Mark H. Senter III, "Emerging Models of Youth Ministry," in *Reaching a Generation for Christ: A Comprehensive Guide to Youth Ministry*, eds. Richard R. Dunn and Mark H. Senter III (Chicago: Moody, 1997); Mark H. Senter III, Wesley Black, Chap Clark, and Malan Nel, *Four Views on Youth Ministry: Inclusive Congregational, Prepatory, Missional, Strategic* (El Cajon, Calif.: Youth Specialties Academic, 2001); and Chap Clark, ed., *Youth Ministry in the 21st Century: Five Views* (Grand Rapids, Mich.: Baker Academic, 2015).

3 See Mark DeVries, *Family-Based Youth Ministry*, rev. and exp. (Downers Grove, Ill.: IVP, 2004); Doug Fields, *Purpose-Driven Youth Ministry: 9 Essential Foundations for Healthy Growth*, Youth Specialties, 2nd ed. (Grand Rapids, Mich.: Zondervan, 2013); and Rick Lawrence, *Jesus Centered Youth Ministry: Moving From Jesus-Plus to Jesus-Only*, rev. ed. (Loveland, Colo.: Simply Youth Ministry, 2014).

Each of these models offers helpful corrections and/or discussion to the practice of youth ministry. I simply use these books as examples of the various models available. However, I disagree with Chap Clark, who believes that there's a distinct difference between a "theology of ministry" and a "structural philosophy." Chap Clark, ed., *Youth Ministry in the 21st Century: Five Views* (Grand Rapids, Mich.: Baker Academic, 2015), xv. While a youth pastor may begin with one or the other, they're intrinsically linked. One's theology of ministry affects one's philosophy of ministry, and vice versa.

4 See Andrew Root, *Bonhoeffer as Youth Worker: A Theological Vision for Discipleship and Life Together* (Grand Rapids, Mich.: Baker Academic, 2014), 4-5.

5 DeVries, *Sustainable Youth Ministry*, 10.

6 See R. Kent and Barbara Hughes, *Liberating Ministry from the Success Syndrome* (Wheaton, Ill.: Crossway, 2008).

7 DeVries, *Sustainable Youth Ministry*, 19.

8 Dietrich Bonhoeffer, *Life Together* (San Francisco: Harper San Francisco, 1954), 27-28.

9 Chap Clark, ed. *Youth Ministry in the 21st Century: Five Views* (Grand Rapids, Mich.: Baker Academic, 2015), xiii.

10 Duffy Robbins, *This Way to Youth Ministry: An Introduction to the Adventure* (El Cajon, Calif.: Youth Specialties Academic, 2004), 19.

11 Ibid., 18-19.

12 Richard R. Dunn, "A Theological Framework for Doing Youth Ministry," in *Reaching a Generation for Christ: A Comprehensive Guide to Youth Ministry*, eds. Richard R. Dunn and Mark H. Senter III (Chicago: Moody, 1997), 46.

13 Robbins, 20.
14 Ibid., 19
15 See J. I. Packer, *Knowing God* (1973; repr., Downers Grove, Ill.: IVP, 1993).
16 I'm indebted to this distinction made by Cameron Cole. See Cameron Cole and Jon Nielson, eds., *Gospel-Centered Youth Ministry: A Practical Guide* (Wheaton, Ill.: Crossway, 2016), 26.
17 Dean Borgman, *Foundations for Youth Ministry: Theological Engagement with Teen Life and Culture* (Grand Rapids, Mich.: Baker Academic, 2013), 3.
18 Italics added.
19 Wayne Rice, *Reinventing Youth Ministry (Again): From Bells and Whistles to Flesh and Blood* (Downers Grove, Ill.: InterVarsity, 2010), 65.

Chapter 3

1 Martin Luther; quoted in Martin Albrecht, "The Effects of Luther's Catechisms on the Church of the Sixteenth Century" (lecture, Dr. Martin Luther College and Wisconsin Lutheran Seminary, 1979); http:www.wlsessays.net/authors/A/AlbrechtEffects/AlbrechtEffects.PDF; accessed August 14, 2007; quoted in Kenda Creasy Dean, *Almost Christian: What the Faith of Our Teenagers is Telling the American Church* (New York: Oxford University Press, 2010), 111.
2 Stuart Cummings-Bond, "The One-Eared Mickey Mouse," *Youthworker* (Fall 1989): 76.
3 Thomas Bergler, *The Juvenilization of American Christianity* (Grand Rapids, Mich.: Eerdmans, 2012), 205, 208.
4 G. A. Pritchard, *Willow Creek Seeker Services: Evaluating a New Way of Doing Church* (Grand Rapids, Mich.: Baker, 1996), 33; quoted in Warren Cole Smith, *A Lover's Quarrel with the Evangelical Church* (Colorado Springs: Authentic, 2008), 76.
5 Andrew Root and Kenda Creasy Dean, *The Theological Turn in Youth Ministry* (Downers Grove, Ill.: Intervarsity, 2011), 31.
6 See Melanie Ross, "The Search for a Grown-up Youth Culture," *Yale University: Reflections; A Magazine of Theological and Ethical Inquiry from Yale Divinity School*, 2014; http://reflections.yale.edu/article/seeking-light-new-generation/search-grown-youth-culture; accessed March 21, 2015; Internet.
7 See Thomas E. Bergler, *The Juvenilization of American Christianity* (Grand Rapids, Mich.: Eerdmans, 2012).
8 Ronald White, "History of Youth Ministry Project" (unpublished mid-project report submitted to the Lilly Endowment, Indianapolis, Ind., August 20, 1994), 7; quoted in Root and Dean, 29.
9 Root and Dean, 16-17.
10 Chap Clark, "Adoptive Youth Ministry: A New Typology for the Theological Grounding of Youth Ministry Practice," *The Journal of Youth Ministry*, vol. 14, no. 2 (Spring 2016): 18.
11 Historically, the church has used catechism, or catechesis, to instruct both the young and new converts. Essentially, catechisms are pedagogical tools used for teaching the foundational truths of the faith. See J. I. Packer and

Gary A. Parrett, *Grounding in the Gospel: Building Believers the Old-Fashioned Way* (Grand Rapids, Mich.: Baker, 2010).

12 Andrew Root, *Bonhoeffer as Youth Worker: A Theological Vision for Discipleship and Life Together* (Grand Rapids, Mich.: Baker Academic, 2014), 4-5.

13 Mark H. Senter, *When God Shows Up: A History of Protestant Youth Ministry in America* (Grand Rapids, Mich.: Baker Academic, 2010), 309.

14 Christian Smith and Patricia Snell, *Souls in Transition: The Religious and Spiritual Lives of Emerging Adults* (New York: Oxford University Press, 2009), 299.

15 Root and Dean, 31.

16 Jonny Baker, "Youth Ministry Changes More than You Know," in *Global Youth Ministry: Reaching Adolescents Around the World*, eds. Terry Linhart and David Livermore (Grand Rapids, Mich.: Zondervan, 2011), 43.

17 Tom Bergler, "Don't Leave Home Without Your Map! Essential History for Youth Ministers," in Duffy Robbins, *This Way to Youth Ministry: An Introduction to the Adventure* (El Cajon, Calif.: Youth Specialties Academic, 2004), 441.

Chapter 4

1 Alvin Reid, *As You Go: Creating a Missional Culture of Gospel-Centered Students* (Colorado Springs: THINK, 2013), 49.

2 A. W. Tozer, *The Knowledge of the Holy* (New York: HarperOne, 1961), 1.

3 Richard Ross, *Student Ministry and the Supremacy of Christ* (Bloomington, Ind.: Cross, 2009), 7.

4 See Christian Smith, "On 'Moralistic Therapeutic Deism' as U.S. Teenagers' Actual, Tacit, De Facto Religious Faith," *Princeton Theological Seminary*; https://www.ptsem.edu/uploadedFiles/School_of_Christian_Vocation_and_Mission/Institute_for_Youth_Ministry/Princeton_Lectures/Smith-Moralistic.pdf; accessed June 10, 2015; Internet. See also Christian Smith and Melinda Lundquist Denton, *Soul Searching: The Religious and Spiritual Lives of American Teenagers* (Oxford: Oxford University Press, 2005), 118-71.

5 Smith, "On 'Moralistic Therapeutic Deism' as U.S. Teenagers' Actual Tacit, De Facto Religious Faith," 46-47.

6 Richard Ross, "The Youth Leader and King Jesus," *Journal for Baptist Theology and Ministry*, vol. 13, no. 1 (Spring 2016): 22.

7 C. S. Lewis, *Mere Christianity* (New York: HarperCollins, 1980), 118.

8 Reid, 47.

9 Ibid., 49.

10 Alan Stewart, ed., *No Guts, No Glory: How to Build a Youth Ministry That Lasts* (Kingsford, NSW, Australia: Matthias Media, 2000), 72.

11 David Hertweck, "The Sucker's Choice: Is It Either/Or . . . or . . . Both/And?" *Doug Fields: Marriage, Family, Youth Ministry, Leadership*, August 31, 2012; http://www.dougfields.com/posts/the-suckers-choice-is-it-eitheror-or-bothand/; quoted in Greg Stier, "The Gospel Advancing View of Youth Ministry," in *Youth Ministry in the 21st Century: Five Views*, ed. Chap Clark (Grand Rapids, Mich.: Baker Academic, 2015), 10.

12 Stier, 12.

13 Ibid., 5.

14 Stephen Ingram, "From Objects of Mission to Agents of Mission," in *Letters to a Youth Worker*, ed. Mark Devries (Nashville: CYMT, 2012), 53.

15 Reid, 21.

16 F. Leroy Forlines, "Critique of the Hybels Seeker Service" (unpublished manuscript, June 1994), 2.

17 For more, see Christopher Wright, *The Mission of God's People: A Biblical Theology of the Church's Mission* (Grand Rapids, Mich.: Zondervan, 2010); and Timothy Keller, *Ministries of Mercy: The Call of the Jericho Road* (Phillipsburg, N.J.: P&R, 2015).

Chapter 5

1 Brian H. Cosby, *Giving Up Gimmicks: Reclaiming Youth Ministry from an Entertainment Culture* (Phillipsburg, N.J.: P&R, 2012), 18.

2 See J. Matthew Pinson, *The Washing of the Saints' Feet* (Nashville: Randall House, 2006).

3 See Alan Stewart, ed., *No Guts, No Glory: Building a Youth Ministry that Lasts* (Kingsford, NSW, Australia: Matthias Media, 2000), 17.

4 Thomas E. Bergler, *The Juvenilization of American Christianity* (Grand Rapids, Mich.: Eerdmans, 2012), 53.

5 See Cosby, 63. A significant portion of this chapter, and even this book, is indebted to Brian Cosby and his writing on this subject. Through *Giving up Gimics* and his contributions in other writings, he has made a significant impact on my own ministry. I appreciate his work on synthesizing the sufficiency of Scripture, the regulative principle, and contemporary youth ministry practice.

6 See Cosby.

7 Bergler, 51.

8 Cosby, 18

9 Cosby notes that the Word, ordinances (what he refers to as sacraments), and prayer are the historical means. Ministry and discipleship follow later. He makes this dichotomy as a result of the Westminster Larger Catechism, Question 154. See Cosby, 24.

10 Cosby, 24. I'm thankful to Cosby for this clarification. This is a term used in Roman Catholic theology referring to the supernatural work of the sacraments, regardless of the participant's activity and/or disposition. Roman Catholics believe that the sacraments confer special grace when performed with no condition on the participant.

11 Ibid.

12 Italics added.

13 Cosby, 26.

14 Fred P. Edie, *Book, Bath, Table and Time: Christian Worship as a Source and Resource for Youth Ministry* (Cleveland: Pilgrim, 2007), 2.

15 Ibid., 5.

16 A quotation similar to this appears in *Shadowlands*, directed by Richard Attenborough (1993; Hollywood, Calif.: Paramount Pictures, 1994), VHS. To read Lewis's thoughts on prayer, see C. S. Lewis, *Letters to Malcolm, Chiefly on Prayer* (New York: HarperOne, 2017).

17 John Bunyan, *Prayer*, Puritan Paperbacks (Carlisle, Penn.: The Banner of Truth Trust, 2012), 13.
18 Donald S. Whitney, *Spiritual Disciplines for the Christian Life* (Colorado Springs: NavPress, 1991), 116.
19 Pinson, 28.

Chapter 6

1 Francis A. Schaeffer, *The God Who Is There* (Downers Grove, Ill.: IVP, 1968); in *The Francis A. Schaeffer Trilogy* (Wheaton, Ill.: Crossway, 1990), 153.
2 Leroy Forlines, "Understanding Yourself and Others: A Biblical, Theological, and Practical Approach to Personality" (unpublished manuscript, 1994) 7-8.
3 The following are helpful primers for the new atheism: R. Albert Mohler, Jr., *Atheism Remix: A Christian Confronts the New Atheists* (Wheaton, Ill.: Crossway, 2008); and Ravi Zacharias, *The End of Reason: A Response to the New Atheists* (Grand Rapids, Mich.: Zondervan, 2008).
4 Larry Alex Taunton, "Listening to Young Atheists: Lessons for a Stronger Christianity," *The Atlantic*, June 6, 2013; http://www.theatlantic.com/national/archive/2013/06/listening-to-young-atheists-lessons-for-a-stronger-christianity/276584/; accessed September 14, 2015; Internet.
5 Walt Mueller, *Engaging the Soul of Youth Culture: Bridging Teen Worldviews and Christian Truth* (Downers Grove, Ill.: IVP, 2006), 80-81.
6 Dividing apologetics between the schools of evidentialism and presuppositionalism is an over-simplification. Nevertheless, experts differ as to their precise number. See Steven B. Cowan, ed., *Five Views on Apologetics* (Grand Rapids, Mich.: Zondervan, 2000); Peter Kreeft and Ronald K. Tacelli, *Handbook of Christian Apologetics* (Downers Grove, Ill.: IVP, 1994); Norman L. Geisler, *Christian Apologetics*, 2nd ed. (Grand Rapids, Mich.: Baker Academic, 2013); and William Lane Craig, *Apologetics: An Introduction* (Chicago: Moody, 1984).
7 Cowan, 16. The evidential and classical schools share much in common.
8 The evidential approach to apologetics suffers from a modernistic mindset, focusing heavily on an empirical epistemology. Today, however, we must account for our postmodern epistemologies.
9 Cowan, 18-19.
10 John Frame, "Presuppositional Apologetics," in Cowan, 220.
11 See Schaeffer, *The God Who Is There*, ch. 2.
12 Forlines uses the same approach to worldview and knowledge; see F. Leroy Forlines, *The Quest for Truth: Answering Life's Inescapable Questions* (Nashville: Randall House, 2001), ch. 7. See also Ronald H. Nash, *Worldviews in Conflict: Choosing Christianity in the World of Ideas* (Grand Rapids, Mich.: Zondervan, 1992); and Edward John Carnell, *Introduction to Christian Apologetics: A Philosophical Defense of the Trinitarian-Theistic Faith*, 6th ed. (Grand Rapids, Mich.: Eerdmans, 1948; repr., Alhambra, Calif.: Green Leaf, 1997). These books offer an approach of testing worldviews to see which one offers the most cohesive, consistent, and satisfying answer to life's inescapable questions.

13 Evidentialists rarely work exclusively in evidences. Likewise, presuppositionalists don't discount the use of evidences. Nevertheless, these categories are helpful when developing a framework for teaching and facilitating apologetics.

14 Schaeffer, *The God Who Is There*, 120.

15 Louis Markos, *Apologetics for the 21st Century* (Wheaton, Ill.: Crossway, 2010), 19-20.

16 Schaeffer, *The God Who Is There*, 155.

17 Ibid.

18 Brock Morgan, *Youth Ministry in a Post-Christian World: A Hopeful Wake-Up Call* (San Diego: Youth Cartel, 2013), 80.

19 Morgan writes, "If we become Christian relativists and embrace tolerance, won't that leads kids to reject the faith? Doesn't that mean we're saying there's no absolute truth? Doesn't this devalue the authority of Scripture? Won't this lead to a free-for-all where people can believe anything they want to believe?' I hear you. My first response is this: Post-Christian kids are already there. . . . I mean, what if you're wrong about that one theological issue that you believe is so vital?" (82-83)

20 Cornelius Van Til, *Christian Apologetics* (Phillipsburg, N.J.: P&R, 2003), 20-54. Van Til argues that apologetics, rather than functioning as its own discipline, should function across all theological disciplines.

21 Francis A. Schaeffer, *The Mark of the Christian*, IVP Classics (Downers Grove, Ill.: InterVarsity, 2006), 26.

22 Schaeffer, *The God Who Is There*, 125.

Chapter 7

1 *Publications of the Colonial Society of Massachusetts*, vol. 21 (Boston: The Colonial Society of Massachusetts, 1920): 259-65; quoted in Michael and Michelle Anthony, *A Theology for Family Ministries* (Nashville: B&H, 2011), 161.

2 See Andreas J. Köstenberger with David W. Jones, *God, Marriage, and the Family: Rebuilding the Biblical Foundation,* 2nd ed. (Wheaton, Ill.: Crossway, 2010), 252-53.

3 See Scottie May, et al., *Children Matter: Celebrating Their Place in the Church, Family and Community* (Grand Rapids, Mich.: Eerdmans, 2005), 165-66.

4 Timothy Paul Jones and John David Trentham, eds., *Practical Family Ministry: A Collection of Ideas for Your Church* (Nashville: Randall House, 2015), 13.

5 Köstenberger with Jones, 85.

6 Vigen Guroian, "The Ecclesial Family: John Chrysostom on Parenthood and Children," in *The Child and Christian Thought*, ed. Marcia J. Bunge (Grand Rapids, Mich.: Eerdmans, 2001), 61-62; italics added.

7 Mark DeVries, *Family-based Youth Ministry*, rev. and exp. (Downers Grove, Ill.: Intervarsity, 2004), 61.

8 *A Treatise of the Faith and Practices of the National Association of Free Will Baptists* (Nashville: Executive Office, National Association of Free Will Baptists, 2008), 1; italics added.

9 The preceding two paragraphs are adapted from Donald S. Whitney, *Family Worship* (Wheaton, Ill.: Crossway, 2016). Concerning a storybook Bible,

I recommend Sally Lloyd-Jones, *The Jesus Story-book Bible* (Grand Rapids, Mich.: ZonderKidz, 2007).

10 Christopher Shlect, *Critique of Modern Youth Ministry*, 2nd ed. (Moscow, Ida.: Canon, 2007), 17.

11 DeVries, *Family-based Youth Ministry*, 87.

12 May, 170.

13 Timothy Paul Jones, "Introduction," in *Practical Family Ministry: A Collection of Ideas for Your Church*, eds. Timothy Paul Jones and John David Trentham (Nashville: Randall House, 2015), 12.

14 Ibid.

15 For those interested in the struggles of intergenerational discipleship, youth culture, and authority, see my article, "Let No One Despise You for Your Elders: The Resolution of Youthful Rebellion and Elder Authority as Found in 1 Timothy," *D6 Family Ministry Journal*, vol. 1 (2016): 149-61.

16 Mark DeVries, *Sustainable Youth Ministry: Why Most Youth Ministry Doesn't Last and What Your Church Can Do About It* (Downers Grove, Ill.: InterVarsity, 2008), 144.

17 See *Adoptive Youth Ministry: Integrating Emerging Generations into the Family of Faith*, ed. Chap Clark (Grand Rapids, Mich.: Baker Academic, 2016).

18 Kara E. Powell, Brad M. Griffin, and Cheryl A. Crawford, *Sticky Faith: Youth Worker Edition: Practical Ideas to Nurture Long-term Faith in Teenagers* (Grand Rapids, Mich.: Zondervan, 2011), 75.

19 DeVries, *Family-based Youth Ministry*, 103.

Chapter 8

1 J. R. R. Tolkien, *The Fellowship of the Ring*, 2nd ed. (Boston: Houghton Mifflin, 1965), 60.

2 Doug Fields, *Your First Two Years in Youth Ministry: A Personal and Practical Guide to Starting Right* (Grand Rapids, Mich.: Zondervan, 2002), 235.

3 Ibid., 247.

4 Mark H. Senter III, "Axioms of Youth Ministry: The Context," in *Reaching a Generation for Christ: A Comprehensive Guide to Youth Ministry*, eds. Richard R. Dunn and Mark H. Senter III (Chicago: Moody, 1997), 134.

5 Colin Marshall and Tony Payne, *The Trellis and the Vine: The Ministry Mind-Shift That Changes Everything* (Kingsford, NSW, Australia: Matthias Media, 2009), 8.

6 Ibid.

7 Ibid.

8 Mark DeVries, *Sustainable Youth Ministry: Why Most Youth Ministry Doesn't Last and What Your Church Can Do About It* (Downers Grove, Ill.: InterVarsity, 2008), 53.

9 No national consensus exists with this study; in fact, this statistic differs from denomination to denomination.

10 David Schroeder, "Leading as a Servant," in *Impact: Student Ministry That Will Transform a Generation*, ed. Steven Patty, TruthQuest, gen. ed. Steven Keels (Nashville: Broadman and Holman, 2005), 274

11 Josh Branum, "Personal Holiness and Evangelistic Leadership: Understanding the Relationship Between Practicing Spiritual Disciplines and Effective Student Evangelism," *The Journal of Youth Ministry,* vol. 15, no. 1 (Fall 2016): 10.

12 DeVries, 44.

13 Ron Hunter, Jr. *The DNA of D6: Building Blocks of Generational Discipleship* (Nashville: Randall House, 2015), 112.

14 DeVries, 83.

15 Italics added.

16 DeVries, 56.

17 Tim Schmoyer, *Life in Student Ministry: Practical Conversations on Thriving in Youth Ministry* (Grand Rapids, Mich.: Zondervan, 2011), 143.

Chapter 9

1 Jonathan Leeman, *Reverberation: How God's Word Brings Light, Freedom, and Action to His People* (Wheaton, Ill.: Moody, 2011), 19.

2 See Timothy Keller, *Preaching: Communicating Faith in an Age of Skepticism* (New York: Penguin, 2015), 1-7. Keller argues for three levels of "word ministry": (1) admonition; (2) counseling, instructing, teaching, or evangelizing; and (3) sermons.

3 See John Stott, *Between Two Worlds: The Challenge of Preaching Today* (Grand Rapids, Mich.: Eerdmans, 1982).

4 Ibid., 138.

5 Gregory C. Carlson, *Rock Solid Teacher: Discover the Joy of Teaching Like Jesus* (Ventura, Calif.: Gospel Light, 2006), 8.

6 See "Chapter Nine: The Pattern: HBLT Approach," in Lawrence O. Richards and Gary J. Bredfelt, *Creative Bible Teaching* (Chicago: Moody, 1998).

7 See "Section 2: How to Create Messages that S.T.I.C.K.," in Doug Fields and Duffy Robbins, *Speaking to Teenagers: How to Think About, Create, and Deliver Effective Messages* (El Cajon, Calif.: Youth Specialties, 2007).

8 This is a woefully short summary of biblical interpretation. I encourage the reader to consider any of a number of accessible books on interpretation, such as Henry A. Virkler and Karelynne Ayayo, *Hermeneutics: Principles and Processes of Biblical Interpretation* (Grand Rapids, Mich.: Baker Academic, 2007); Howard G. Hendricks and William D. Hendricks *Living by the Book: The Art and Science of Reading the Bible* (Chicago: Moody, 2007); and J. Scott Duvall and J. Daniel Hays, *Grasping God's Word: A Hands-On Approach to Reading, Interpreting and Applying God's Word* (Grand Rapids, Mich.: Zondervan, 2012).

9 Haddon W. Robinson, *Biblical Preaching: The Development and Delivery of Expository Messages,* 2nd ed. (Grand Rapids, Mich.: Baker Academic, 2001), 73-74.

10 Keller, 70.

11 See Walter C. Kaiser, Jr., *The Promise-Plan of God: A Biblical Theology of the Old and New Testaments* (Grand Rapids, Mich.: Zondervan, 2008).

12 Robinson, 73.

13 Abraham Kuyper, *Lectures on Calvinism* (Grand Rapids, Mich.: Eerdmans, 1931), 51.

14 James D. Bratt, ed., *Abraham Kuyper: A Centennial Reader* (Grand Rapids, Mich.: Eerdmans, 1998), 488.
15 As with all books, be sure to read these books with a discerning eye. Although I strongly disagree with some parts of them, nonetheless they offer helpful observations about current youth culture and life.
16 Taken from "Welcome to Their Jungle," in Walt Mueller, *Engaging the Soul of Youth Culture: Bridging Teen Worldviews and Christian Truth* (Downers Grove, Ill.: IVP, 2006).
17 See Cameron Cole, "The Gospel at the Heart of All Things: Youth Ministry Founded in the Gospel," in *Gospel-Centered Youth Ministry: A Practical Guide*, eds. Cameron Cole and Jon Nielson (Wheaton, Ill.: Crossway, 2016).
18 Stott, 147.
19 Francis A. Schaeffer, *He Is There And He Is Not Silent* (Carol Stream, Ill.: Tyndale House, 1972); in *The Francis A. Schaeffer Trilogy* (Wheaton, Ill.: Crossway, 1990), 153.

Chapter 10

1 Neil Postman, "Informing Ourselves to Death," in *The Nature of Technology: Implications for Learning and Teaching*, eds. Michael P. Clough, Joanne K. Olson, and Dale S. Niederhauser (Boston: Sense, 2013), 9.
2 Gijsbert van der Wal, "Nieuwe generatie museumbezoekers vanmiddag in het," November 27, 2014, 3:44pm; Tweet; https://twitter.com/wijdopenogen/status/538085905987567616.
3 See Andrew Root, *Bonhoeffer as Youth Worker: A Theological Vision for Discipleship and Life Together* (Grand Rapids, Mich.: Baker Academic, 2014), 4-5.
4 See Marc Prensky, "Digital Natives, Digital Immigrants," *On the Horizon*, vol. 9, no. 5 (October 2001).
5 Marva J. Dawn, *Is It A Lost Cause? Having the Heart of God for the Church's Children* (Grand Rapids, Mich.: Eerdmans, 1997), 166-71.
6 In *Everyday Theology*, Kevin Vanhoozer argues that all cultural items (or "texts" as he says) achieve four basic functions: (1) communicate, (2) orients, (3) reproduces, and (4) cultivates. See Kevin Vanhoozer, Charles A. Anderson, and Michael J. Sleasman, eds., *Everyday Theology: How to Read Cultural Texts and Interpret Trends* (Grand Rapids, Mich.: Baker Academic, 2007), 27-32.
7 See Nicholas Carr, *The Shallows: What the Internet Is Doing to Our Brains* (New York: W. W. Norton, 2010); Neil Postman, *Amusing Ourselves to Death: Public Discourse in the Age of Show Business* (New York: Penguin, 1985); Richard Weaver, *Ideas Have Consequences* (Chicago: University of Chicago Press, 1948); T. David Gordon, *Why Johnny Can't Preach* (Phillipsburg, N.J.: P&R, 2009); Kenneth A. Myers, *All God's Children and Blue Suede Shoes: Christians and Popular Culture* (Wheaton, Ill.: Crossway, 1989); and Dawn, especially chs. 10-11.
8 Walt Mueller, *Engaging the Soul of Youth Culture: Bridging Teen Worldviews and Christian Truth* (Downers Grove, Ill.: InterVarsity, 2006), 96-97.
9 Frances E. Jensen with Amy Ellis Nutt, *The Teenage Brain: A Neuroscientist's Survival Guide to Raising Adolescents and Young Adults* (New York: Harper, 2015), 209.
10 Ibid.

11 Carr, 3. Carr is not the first to make this argument. Among others, see Marshall McLuhan and Quentin Fiore, *The Medium Is the Massage: An Inventory of Effects*, 9th ed. (Berkeley, Calif.: Gingko, 2001); Postman, *Amusing Ourselves to Death*; and Weaver.

12 Katherine Hayles; quoted in Naomi S. Baron, *Always On: Language in an Online and Mobile World* (Oxford: Oxford University Press, 2008), 204; quoted in Carr, 9.

13 Greg Poppo, "Kids' electronic media use jumps to 53 hours a week," *USA Today*, January 20, 2010; http://usatoday30.usatoday.com/tech/news/2010-01-20-1Avideokids20_ST_N.htm; accessed July 12, 2016; Internet.

14 Gregg Moder, "Approaching Wise Dialogue With Our Technological Test Pilots: Re-Framing the Story of Digital Progress," *The Journal of Youth Ministry*, vol. 15, no. 1 (Fall 2016): 85-86.

15 C. S. Lewis, *Surprised by Joy: The Shape of My Early Life* (San Diego: Harcourt, Brace, Jovanovich, 1966), 207-08.

16 Ibid.

17 C. S. Lewis, *The Four Loves* (New York: Harcourt, 1988), 137.

18 Moder, 101.

19 Nate Morgan Locke, "Identity," *SOUL*, The Good Book Company, dir. Steve Hughes (Surrey, England: Shepperton Studios, 2010), DVD.

20 I'm thankful to Mr. John Carter for this wonderful illustration.

21 C. S. Lewis, "The Weight of Glory," in *The Weight of Glory and other Essays* (Grand Rapids, Mich.: Eerdmans, 1965), 2.

22 C. S. Lewis, *Mere Christianity* (New York: HarperCollins, 1980), 136-37.

Chapter 11

1 Saint Augustine, *Confessions*, trans. Albert C. Outler, trans. rev. Mark Vessey, Barnes & Noble Classics (New York: Barnes & Noble, 2007), 3.

2 Ibid.

3 "The Gospel," *9Marks*; http://www.9marks.org/what-are-the-9marks/the-gospel; accessed November 18, 2013; Internet.

4 Italics added.

5 Augustine; quoted in "Essentials for the Faith that Saves," *Theological Quarterly*, vol. XXI, no. 2 (St. Louis: Concordia/Lutheran Synod of Missouri, April, 1917): 77. In all likelihood, this quotation has actually been falsely attributed to Augustine.

6 R. Albert Mohler, Jr., *Words From the Fire: Hearing the Voice of God in the Ten Commandments* (Chicago: Moody, 2009), 86-87.

7 "Westminster Shorter Catechism," *Center for Reformed Theology and Apologetics*; http://www.reformed.org/documents/WSC.html; accessed May 25, 2017; Internet

Conclusion

1 Andrew Zirchsky, "Get Trained," in *Letters to a Youth Worker*, ed. Mark DeVries (Brentwood, Tenn.: Center for Youth Ministry Training, 2012), 65.

BIBLIOGRAPHY

A Treatise of the Faith and Practices of the National Association of Free Will Baptist. Nashville: Executive Office of the National Association of Free Will Baptists, 2008.

Allison, Gregg R. *Sojourners and Strangers: The Doctrine of the Church*. Foundations of Evangelical Theology, edited by John S. Feinberg. Wheaton, Ill.: Crossway, 2012.

Anthony, Michael, and Michelle Anthony. *A Theology for Family Ministries*. Nashville: B&H Academic, 2011.

Ashford, Bruce. *Every Square Inch: An Introduction to Cultural Engagement for Christians*. Bellingham, Wash.: Lexham, 2015.

Augustine. *Confessions*. Barnes & Noble Classics. Translated by Albert C. Outler. Translation revised by Mark Vessey. New York: Barnes & Noble, 2007.

Baker, Dori Grinenko, and Joyce Ann Mercer. *Lives to Offer: Accompanying Youth on Their Vocational Quests*. Youth Ministry Alternatives. Cleveland: Pilgrim, 2007.

Baron, Naomi S. *Always On: Language in an Online and Mobile World*. Oxford: Oxford University Press, 2008.

Barrick, Audrey. "Youth Ministries Teaching Behavior Modification, Not the Gospel?" *The Christian Post: Church and Ministries*, April 17, 2012. http://www.christianpost.com/news/youth-ministries-teaching-behavior-modification-not-gospel-73408/. Accessed October 11, 2016. Internet.

Bass, Dorothy C., and Don C. Richter, eds. *Way to Live: Christian Practices for Teens*. Nashville: Upper Room, 2002.

Baucham, Jr., Voddie. *Family Driven Faith: Doing What It Takes to Raise Sons and Daughters Who Walk With God*. Wheaton, Ill.: Crossway, 2007.

———. *Family Shepherds: Calling and Equipping Men to Lead Their Homes*. Wheaton, Ill.: Crossway, 2011.

Benson, Warren S., and Mark H. Senter III, eds. *The Complete Book of Youth Ministry*. Chicago: Moody, 1987.

Bergler, Thomas E. *From Here to Maturity: Overcoming the Juvenilization of American Christianity*. Grand Rapids, Mich.: Eerdmans, 2014.

———. *The Juvenilization of American Christianity*. Grand Rapids, Mich.: Eerdmans, 2012.

Bonhoeffer, Dietrich. *Life Together*. San Francisco: Harper San Francisco, 1954.

Borgman, Dean. *Foundations for Youth Ministry: Theological Engagement with Teen Life and Culture*. 2nd ed. Grand Rapids, Mich.: Baker Academic, 2013.

———. *Hear My Story: Understanding the Cries of Troubled Youth*. Peabody, Mass.: Hendrickson, 2003.

Branum, Josh. "Personal Holiness and Evangelistic Leadership: Understanding the Relationship Between Practicing Spiritual Disciplines and Effective Student Evangelism." *The Journal Of Youth Ministry* 15, no. 1 (Fall 2016): 8-32.

Bratt, James D., ed. *Abraham Kuyper: A Centennial Reader*. Grand Rapids, Mich.: Eerdmans, 1998.

Bunge, Marcia J., ed. *The Child and Christian Thought*. Religion, Marriage and Family (RMF). Grand Rapids, Mich.: Eerdmans, 2001.

Bunyan, John. *Prayer*. Puritan Paperbacks. Carlisle, Penn.: The Banner of Truth Trust, 2012.

Cannister, Mark. *Teenagers Matter: Making Student Ministry a Priority in the Church*. Youth, Family, and Culture, edited by Chap Clark. Grand Rapids, Mich.: Baker Academic, 2013.

Carlson, Gregory C. *Rock Solid Teacher: Discover the Joy of Teaching Like Jesus*. Ventura, Calif.: Gospel Light, 2006.

Carnell, Edward John. *Introduction to Christian Apologetics: A Philosophical Defense of the Trinitarian-Theistic Faith*. 6th ed. Grand Rapids, Mich.: Eerdmans, 1948; repr., Alhambra, Calif.: Green Leaf, 1997.

Carr, Abby. "Youth Groups Driving Christian Teens to Abandon Faith," *Charisma News*, October 22, 2013. http://www.charismanews.com/us/41465-youth-groups-driving-christian-teens-to-abandon-faith. Accessed July 15, 2016. Internet.

Carr, Nicholas. *The Shallows: What the Internet Is Doing to Our Brains*. New York: W. W. Norton, 2010.

Chediak, Alex. *Preparing Your Teens for College: Faith, Friends, Finances, and Much More*. Carol Stream, Ill.: Tyndale, 2014.

Chromey, Rick. *Youth Ministry in Small Churches: Creative How-Tos, Plus 28 Innovative Activities*. Loveland, Colo.: Group, 1990.

Clark, Chap. "Adoptive Youth Ministry: A New Typology for the Theological Grounding of Youth Ministry Practice." *The Journal of Youth Ministry*, vol. 14, no. 2 (Spring 2016): 17-29.

———, ed. *Adoptive Youth Ministry: Integrating Emerging Generations into the Family of Faith*. Youth, Family, and Culture. Grand Rapids, Mich.: Baker Academic, 2016.

———. *Hurt 2.0: Inside the World of Today's Teenagers*. Youth, Family, and Culture. Grand Rapids, Mich.: Baker Academic, 2011.

———, ed. *Youth Ministry in the 21st Century: Five Views*. Youth, Family, and Culture. Grand Rapids, Mich.: Baker Academic, 2015.

Clough, Michael P., Joanne K. Olson, and Dale S. Niederhauser, eds. *The Nature of Technology: Implications for Learning and Teaching*. Boston: Sense, 2013.

Cole, Cameron. "Busy All the Time: Over-Scheduled Children and the Freedom of the Gospel," *The Gospel Coalition*, January 12, 2014. https://www.thegospelcoalition.org/article/busy-all-the-time/. Accessed November 10, 2016. Internet.

Cole, Cameron, and Jon Nielson, eds. *Gospel-Centered Youth Ministry: A Practical Guide*. Wheaton, Ill.: Crossway, 2016.

Coppenger, Mark. *Moral Apologetics for Contemporary Christians: Pushing Back Against Cultural and Religious Critics*. B&H Studies in Christian Ethics. Nashville: B&H, 2011.

Cosby, Brian H. *Giving Up Gimmicks: Reclaiming Youth Ministry from an Entertainment Culture*. Phillipsburg, N.J.: P&R, 2012.

Cowan, Steven B., ed. *Five Views on Apologetics*. Counterpoints: Bible and

Theology, edited by Stanley N. Gundry. Grand Rapids, Mich.: Zondervan, 2000.

Craig, William Lane. *Apologetics: An Introduction*. Chicago: Moody, 1984.

Cummings-Bond, Stuart. "The One-Eared Mickey Mouse," *Youthworker* (Fall 1989).

Dawn, Marva J. *Is It A Lost Cause? Having the Heart of God for the Church's Children*. Grand Rapids, Mich.: Eerdmans, 1997.

Dean, Kenda Creasy. *Almost Christian: What the Faith of Our Teenagers Is Telling the American Church*. New York: Oxford University Press, 2010.

Detweiler, Craig. *iGods: How Technology Shapes Our Spiritual and Social Lives*. Grand Rapids, Mich.: Brazos, 2013.

Dever, Mark, and Greg Gilbert. *Preach: Theology Meets Practice*. 9Marks. Nashville: B&H, 2012.

DeVries, Mark. *Family-based Youth Ministry*. Rev. and exp. ed. Downers Grove, Ill.: InterVarsity, 2004.

———, ed. *Letters to a Youth Worker*. Brentwood, Tenn.: Center for Youth Ministry Training, 2012.

———. *Sustainable Youth Ministry: Why Most Youth Ministry Doesn't Last and What Your Church Can Do About It*. Downers Grove, Ill.: IVP, 2008.

Dunn, Richard R., and Mark H. Senter III, eds. *Reaching a Generation for Christ: A Comprehensive Guide to Youth Ministry*. Rev. ed. Chicago: Moody, 1997.

Duvall, J. Scott, and J. Daniel Hays. *Grasping God's Word: A Hands-On Approach to Reading, Interpreting and Applying God's Word*. 3rd ed. Grand Rapids, Mich.: Zondervan, 2012.

Edie, Fred P. *Book, Bath, Table and Time: Christian Worship as a Source and Resource for Youth Ministry*. Youth Ministry Alternatives. Cleveland: Pilgrim, 2007.

"Essentials for the Faith that Saves," *Theological Quarterly*, vol. XXI, no. 2 (St. Louis: Concordia/Lutheran Synod of Missouri, April, 1917).

Fields, Doug. *Purpose-Driven Youth Ministry: 9 Essential Foundations for Healthy Growth*. Youth Specialties. 2nd ed. Grand Rapids, Mich.: Zondervan, 2013.

———. *Your First Two Years in Youth Ministry: A Personal and Practical Guide to Starting Right*. Grand Rapids, Mich.: Zondervan/Youth Specialties, 2002.

Fields, Doug, and Duffy Robbins. *Speaking to Teenagers: How to Think About, Create, and Deliver Effective Messages*. Grand Rapids, Mich.: Zondervan/Youth Specialties, 2007.

"Forever Young," *Mortification of Spin Podcast*, May 27, 2015. http://www.alliancenet.org/mos/podcast/forever-young#.WNp5YjLMyCQ. Accessed January 20, 2017. Internet.

Forlines, Leroy. "Critique of the Hybel's Seeker's Service." Unpublished manuscript, June, 1994.

———. *The Quest for Truth: Answering Life's Inescapable Questions*. Nashville: Randall House, 2001.

———. "Understanding Yourself and Others: A Biblical, Theological, and Practical Approach to Personality." Unpublished manuscript, 1994.

Forster, Greg. *Joy for the World: How Christianity Lost Its Cultural Influence and Can Begin Rebuilding It*. Wheaton, Ill.: Crossway, 2014

Gage, Rodney. *Why Your Kids Do What They Do: Responding to the Driving Forces Behind Your Teen's Behavior*. Nashville: B&H, 1999.

Geisler, Norman L. *Christian Apologetics*. 2nd ed. Grand Rapids, Mich.: Baker Academic, 2013.

Gerali, Steven. *What Do I Do When Teenagers Encounter Bullying and Violence?* Grand Rapids, Mich.: Zondervan/Youth Specialties, 2009.

Gilbert, Greg. *What Is the Gospel?* Wheaton, Ill.: Crossway, 2010.

Gordon, T. David. *Why Johnny Can't Preach: The Media Have Shaped the Messengers*. Phillipsburg, N.J.: P&R, 2009.

"The Gospel," *9Marks*, May 15, 2014. http://www.9marks.org/what-are-the-9marks/the-gospel. Accessed November 18 2016. Internet.

Hendricks, Howard G., and William D. Hendricks. *Living by the Book: The Art and Science of Reading the Bible*. 3rd Ed. Chicago: Moody, 2007.

Howard, Mark. "Fun and Substance in Youth Ministry," *Rooted Ministry*, October 20, 2013. https://www.rootedministry.com/blog/fun-and-substance-in-youth-ministry/. Accessed January 12, 2017. Internet.

Hughes, R. Kent, and Barbara Hughes. *Liberating Ministry from the Success Syndrome*. Wheaton, Ill.: Crossway, 2008.

Hull, Bill. *The Complete Book of Discipleship*. Annotated ed. The Navigators Reference Library. Colorado Springs: NavPress, 2006.

Hunter, Jr., Ron. *The DNA of D6: Building Blocks of Generational Discipleship*. Nashville: Randall House, 2015.

Hybels, Bill. *Courageous Leadership: Field-Tested Strategy for the 360° Leader*. Reprint ed. Grand Rapids, Mich.: Zondervan, 2012.

Jensen, Frances E., with Amy Ellis Nutt. *The Teenage Brain: A Neuroscientist's Survival Guide to Raising Adolescents and Young Adults*. Reprint ed. New York: Harper, 2015.

Jones, Timothy Paul. *Family Ministry Field Guide: How Your Church Can Equip Parents to Make Disciples*. Indianapolis, Ind.: Wesleyan Publishing House, 2011.

Jones, Timothy Paul, and John David Trentham, eds. *Practical Family Ministry: A Collection of Ideas for Your Church*. Nashville: Randall House, 2015.

Kaiser, Jr., Walter C. *The Promise-Plan of God: A Biblical Theology of the Old and New Testaments*. Grand Rapids, Mich.: Zondervan, 2008.

Keehn, Dave. "Biblical Mandate for Youth Ministry (Part 3): Youth Ministry in the New Testament," *The Good Book Blog*, March 5, 2012. http://www.thegoodbookblog.com/ 2012/ mar/05/biblical-mandate-for-youth-ministry-part-3-youth-m/. Accessed January 9, 2015. Internet.

"Keeping Our Kids, Part 1," *White Horse Inn Podcast*, May 18, 2014. http://www.whitehorseinn.org /blog/2014/05/18/whi-1206-keeping-our-kids-part-1/. Accessed December 10, 2016. Internet.

"Keeping Our Kids, Part 2," *White Horse Inn Podcast*, May 25, 2015. http://www.whitehorseinn.org /blog/2014/05/25/whi-1207-keeping-our-kids-part-2/. Accessed December 10, 2016. Internet.

Keller, Timothy. *Center Church: Doing Balanced, Gospel-Centered Ministry in Your City*. Grand Rapids, Mich.: Zondervan, 2012.

———. *Ministries of Mercy: The Call of the Jericho Road*. 3rd ed. Phillipsburg, N.J.: P&R, 2015.

———. *Preaching: Communicating Faith in an Age of Skepticism*. Reprint ed. New York: Viking, 2015.

———. *The Reason for God: Belief in an Age of Skepticism*. Reprint ed. New York: Riverhead, 2008.

Kelly, Paul G. "A Theology of Youth." *Journal for Baptist Theology and Ministry*, vol. 13, no. 1 (Spring 2016): 3-19.

Kinnaman, David, with Aly Hawkins. *You Lost Me: Why Young Christians Are Leaving Church . . . And Rethinking Faith*. Grand Rapids, Mich.: Baker, 2011.

Kipp, Mike. "Is 'Youth Ministry' in the Bible? Researching the Scripture Behind Youth and Family Ministry," *Fuller Youth Institute*, July 30, 2012. http://fulleryouthinstitute.org/articles/is-youth-ministry-in-the-bible. Accessed January 9, 2015. Internet.

Köstenberger, Andreas J., with David W. Jones. *God, Marriage, and Family: Rebuilding the Biblical Foundation*. 2nd ed. Wheaton, Ill.: Crossway, 2010.

Kreeft, Peter, and Ronald K. Tacelli. *Handbook of Christian Apologetics*. Reprint ed. Downers Grove, Ill.: IVP, 1994.

Kuyper, Abraham, *Lectures on Calvinism*. Grand Rapids, Mich.: Eerdmans, 1931.

Lawrence, Rick. *Jesus Centered Youth Ministry: Moving From Jesus-Plus to Jesus-Only*. Rev. ed. Loveland, Colo.: Simply Youth Ministry, 2014.

Leeman, Jonathan. *Reverberation: How God's Word Brings Light, Freedom, and Action to His People*. 9Marks. Wheaton, Ill.: Moody, 2011.

Lewis, C. S. *Christian Reflections*. Grand Rapids, Mich.: Eerdmans, 2014.

———. *The Four Loves*. New York: Harcourt, 1988.

———. *Letters to Malcolm, Chiefly on Prayer*. New York: HarperOne, 2017.

———. *Mere Christianity*. New York: HarperCollins, 1952.

———. *Surprised by Joy: The Shape of My Early Life*. San Diego: Harcourt, Brace, Jovanovich, 1966.

———. "The Weight of Glory," in *The Weight of Glory and other Essays*. Grand Rapids, Mich.: Eerdmans, 1965.

Linhart, Terry, and David Livermore. *Global Youth Ministry: Reaching Adolescents Around the World*. Grand Rapids, Mich.: Zondervan/Youth Specialties Academic, 2011.

Locke, Nate Morgan. "Identity," *SOUL*, The Good Book Company, directed by Steve Hughes. Surrey, England: Shepperton Studios, 2010. DVD.

Lloyd-Jones, Sally. *The Jesus Story-book Bible*. Grand Rapids, Mich.: ZonderKidz, 2007.

Marcellino, Jerry. *Rediscovering Family Worship*. Wapwallopen, Penn.: Shepherd, 2011.

Markins, Matt, and Dan Lovaglia, with Mark McPeak. *The Gospel Truth About Children's Ministry: 10 Fresh KidMin Research Findings*. Streamwood, Ill.: Awana, 2015.

Markos, Louis. *Apologetics for the 21st Century*. Wheaton, Ill.: Crossway, 2010.

Marshall, Colin, and Tony Payne. *The Trellis and the Vine: The Ministry Mind-Shift that Changes Everything*. Kingsford, NSW, Australia: Matthias Media, 2009.

Matlock, Mark. *Real World Parents: Christian Parenting for Families Living in the Real World*. Grand Rapids, Mich.: Zondervan/Youth Specialties, 2010.

May, Scottie, et al. *Children Matter: Celebrating Their Place in the Church, Family, and Community*. Grand Rapids, Mich.: Eerdmans, 2005.

McConnell, Scott. "LifeWay Research Finds Reasons 18- to 22-Year-Olds Drop Out of Church," *Lifeway.com*, August, 2007. http://www.lifeway.com/ArticleView?storeId=10054&catalogId=10001&langId=-1&article=LifeWay-Research-finds-reasons-18-to-22-year-olds-drop-out-of-church. Accessed February 1, 2013. Internet.

McLuhan, Marshall, and Quentin Fiore. *The Medium Is the Massage: An Inventory of Effects*. 9th ed. Berkeley, Calif.: Gingko, 2001.

McKee, Jonathan. *Connect: Real Relationships in a World of Isolation*. Grand Rapids, Mich.: Zondervan/Youth Specialties, 2009.

McKee, Jonathan, and David R. Smith. *Ministry By Teenagers: Developing Leaders from Within*. Grand Rapids, Mich.: Zondervan/Youth Specialties, 2011.

Moder, Gregg. "Approaching Wise Dialogue With Our Technological Test Pilots: Reframing the Story of Digital Progress." *The Journal Of Youth Ministry* 15, no. 1 (Fall 2016): 85-104.

Mohler, Jr, R. Albert. *Atheism Remix: A Christian Confronts the New Atheists*. Wheaton, Ill.: Crossway, 2008.

———. *Words From the Fire: Hearing the Voice of God in the Ten Commandments*. Chicago: Moody, 2009.

Moore, Russell. *Onward: Engaging the Culture Without Losing the Gospel*. Nashville: B&H, 2015.

Morgan, Brock. *Youth Ministry in a Post-Christian World: A Hopeful Wake-Up Call*. San Diego: Youth Cartel, 2013.

Mueller, Walt. *Engaging the Soul of Youth Culture: Bridging Teen Worldviews and Christian Truth*. Downers Grove, Ill.: IVP, 2006.

———. *Youth Culture 101*. Grand Rapids, Mich.: Zondervan/Youth Specialties, 2007.

Myers, Kenneth A. *All God's Children and Blue Suede Shoes: Christians and Popular Culture*. Wheaton, Ill.: Crossway, 1989.

Nash, Ronald H. *Worldviews in Conflict: Choosing Christianity in the World of Ideas*. Grand Rapids, Mich.: Zondervan, 1992.

Owen, John. *The Glory of Christ*. Puritan Paperback. Carlisle, Penn.: The Banner of Truth Trust, 1994.

Packer, J. I., *Knowing God*. 1973; repr., Downers Grove, Ill.: IVP, 1993.

Packer, J. I., and Gary A. Parrett. *Grounding in the Gospel: Building Believers the Old-Fashioned Way*. Grand Rapids, Mich.: Baker, 2010.

Patty, Steven, ed. *Impact: Student Ministry That Will Transform a Generation*. TruthQuest, edited by Steve Keels. Nashville: B&H, 2005.

Pinson, J. Matthew. *The Washing of the Saints' Feet*. Nashville: Randall House, 2006.

Piper, John. *The Supremacy of God in Preaching*. Grand Rapids, Mich.: Baker, 2004.

Poppo, Greg. "Kids' electronic media use jumps to 53 hours a week," *USA Today: Technology*, January 20, 2010. http://usatoday30.usatoday.com/tech/news/2010-01-20-1Avideokids20_ST_N.htm. Accessed July 12, 2016. Internet.

Postman, Neil. *Amusing Ourselves to Death: Public Discourse in the Age of Show Business*. New York: Penguin, 2005.

Powell, Kara E., Brad M. Griffin, and Cheryl A. Crawford. *Sticky Faith: Youth Worker Edition: Practical Ideas to Nurture Long-term Faith in Teenagers*. Grand Rapids, Mich.: Zondervan, 2011.

Powers, Bruce P., ed. *Christian Education Handbook*. Rev. ed. Nashville: B&H, 1996.

Poythress, Vern Sheridan. *Inerrancy and Worldview: Answering Modern Challenges to the Bible*. Wheaton, Ill.: Crossway, 2012.

———. *Redeeming Science: A God-Centered Approach*. Wheaton, Ill.: Crossway, 2006.

Prensky, Marc. "Digital Natives, Digital Immigrants." *On the Horizon*, MCB University Press, vol. 9, no. 5 (October 2001).

Pritchard, G. A. *Willow Creek Seeker Services: Evaluating a New Way of Doing Church*. Grand Rapids, Mich.: Baker, 1996.

Publications of the Colonial Society of Massachusetts, vol. 21. Boston: The Colonial Society of Massachusetts, 1920.

Reid, Alvin, L. *As You Go: Creating a Missional Culture of Gospel-Centered Students*. Colorado Springs: THINK, 2013.

Rice, Wayne. *Reinventing Youth Ministry (Again): From Bells and Whistles to Flesh and Blood*. Downers Grove, Ill.: InterVarsity, 2010.

Richards, Lawrence O., and Gary J. Bredfeldt. *Creative Bible Teaching*. Rev. ed. Chicago: Moody, 1970.

Rienow, Rob, and Amy Rienow. *Five Reasons for Spiritual Apathy in Teens: What Parents Can Do to Help*. Nashville: Randall House, 2015.

Robbins, Duffy. *This Way to Youth Ministry: An Introduction to the Adventure*. Grand Rapids, Mich.: Zondervan/Youth Specialties Academic, 2004.

Robbinson, Haddon W. *Biblical Preaching: The Development and Delivery of Expository Messages*. 2nd ed. Grand Rapids, Mich.: Baker Academic, 2001.

Rookmaaker, Hans. *Modern Art and the Death of a Culture*. Wheaton, Ill.: Crossway, 1970.

Root, Andrew. *Bonhoeffer as Youth Worker: A Theological Vision for Discipleship and Life Together*. Grand Rapids, Mich.: Baker Academic, 2014.

———. *Relationships Unfiltered: Help for Youth Workers, Volunteers, and Parents on Creating Authentic Relationships*. Grand Rapids, Mich.: Zondervan/Youth Specialties, 2009.

Root, Andrew, and Kenda Creasy Dean. *The Theological Turn in Youth Ministry*. Downers Grove, Ill.: IVP, 2011.

Ross, Melanie. "The Search for a Grown-up Youth Culture." *Yale University: Reflections; A Magazine of Theological and Ethical Inquiry from Yale Divinity School*, 2014. http://reflections.yale.edu/article/seeking-light-new-generation/search-grown-youth-culture. Accessed March 21, 2015. Internet.

———. "The Youth Leader and King Jesus," *Journal for Baptist Theology and Ministry*, vol. 13, no. 1 (Spring 2016): 20-23.

Ross, Richard. *Student Ministry and the Supremacy of Christ*. Bloomington, Ind.: Cross, 2009.

Ryle, J. C. *Thoughts for Young Men*. Carlisle, Penn.: The Banner of Truth Trust, 2016.

Schaeffer, Francis A. *The Francis A. Schaeffer Trilogy*. Wheaton, Ill.: Crossway, 1990.

———. *The God Who Is There*. Downers Grove, Ill.: IVP, 1968.

———. *He Is There And He Is Not Silent*. Carol Stream, Ill.: Tyndale House, 1972.

———. *The Mark of the Christian*. IVP Classics. Downers Grove, Ill.: InterVarsity, 2006.

Schmoyer, Tim. *Life in Student Ministry: Practical Conversations on Thriving in Youth Ministry*. Grand Rapids, Mich.: Zondervan/Youth Specialties, 2011.

Senter III, Mark H. *When God Shows Up: A History of Protestant Youth Ministry in America*. Youth, Family, and Culture, edited by Chap Clark. Grand Rapids, Mich.: Baker Academic, 2010.

Senter III, Mark H., Wesley Black, Chap Clark, and Malan Nel. *Four Views on Youth Ministry: Inclusive Congregational, Prepatory, Missional, Strategic*. Grand Rapids, Mich.: Zondervan/Youth Specialties Academic, 2001.

Shadowlands. Directed by Richard Attenborough. 1993. Hollywood, Calif.: Paramount Pictures, 1994. VHS.

Shlect, Christopher. *Critique of Modern Youth Ministry*. Canon Press Monographs. 2nd ed. Moscow, Ida.: Canon, 2007.

Sire, James W. *The Universe Next Door: A Basic Worldview Catalog*. 5th ed. Downers Grove, Ill.: IVP Academic, 2009.

Smith, Christian. "On 'Moralistic Therapeutic Deism' as U.S. Teenagers' Actual, Tacit, De Facto Religious Faith," *Princeton Theological Seminary*. https://www.ptsem.edu/uploadedFiles/School_of_Christian_Vocation_and_Mission/Institute_for_Youth_Ministry/Princeton_Lectures/Smith-Moralistic.pdf. Accessed June 10, 2015. Internet.

Smith, Christian, and Patricia Snell. *Souls in Transition: The Religious & Spiritual Lives of Emerging Adults*. New York: Oxford University Press, 2009.

Smith, Warren Cole. *A Lover's Quarrel with the Evangelical Church*. Colorado Springs: Authentic, 2008.

Stanley, Andy. *Next Generation Leader: 5 Essentials for Those Who Will Shape the Future*. Colorado Springs: Multnomah, 2006.

Steptoe, Sonja. "How to Get Teens Excited About God," *TIME*, November 2006. http://www.time. com/time/nation/article/0,8599,1553366,00.html. Accessed February 1, 2013. Internet.

Stetzer, Ed. "Are Youth Groups Bad? A Rant on Bad Research," *Christianity Today*, May 19, 2014. http://www.christianitytoday.com/edstetzer/2014/may/are-youth-groups-bad.html. Accessed July 15, 2016. Internet.

Stewart, Alan, ed. *No Guts No Glory: How to Build a Youth Ministry That Lasts*. 2nd ed. Kingsford, NSW, Australia: Matthias Media, 2000.

Stott, John R. W. *Between Two Worlds: The Art of Preaching in the Twentieth Century*. Reprint ed. Grand Rapids, Mich.: Eerdmans, 1982.

Strommen, Merton P. *Five Cries of Youth*. San Francisco: Harper & Row, 1988.

Strommen, Merton, Karen E. Jones, and Dave Rahn. *Youth Ministry That Transforms: A Comprehensive Analysis of the Hopes, Frustrations, and Effectiveness of Today's Youth Workers*. Grand Rapids, Mich.: Zondervan/Youth Specialties Academic, 2001.

Talbot, Christopher. "Let No One Despise You for Your Elders: The Resolution of Youthful Rebellion and Elder Authority as Found in 1 Timothy," *D6 Family Ministry Journal*, vol. 1 (2016): 149-61.

Taunton, Larry Alex. "Listening to Young Atheists: Lessons for a Stronger Christianity," *The Atlantic*, June 6, 2013. http://www.theatlantic.com/national/archive/2013/06/listening-to-young-atheists-lessons-for-a-stronger-christianity/276584/. Accessed September 14, 2015. Internet.

Thigpen, Jonathan. *Teaching Students Not Lessons*. Nashville: Randall House, 2009.

Tolkien, J. R. R. *The Fellowship of the Ring*. 2nd ed. Boston: Houghton Mifflin, 1965.

Tozer, A. W. *The Knowledge of the Holy*. New York: HarperOne, 1961.

Van Til, Cornelius. *Christian Apologetics*. Phillipsburg, N.J.: P&R, 2003.

Vanhoozer, Kevin, Charles A. Anderson, and Michael J. Sleasman, eds. *Everyday Theology: How To Read Cultural Texts and Interpret Trends*. Cultural Exegesis. Grand Rapids, Mich.: Baker Academic, 2007.

Virkler, Henry A., and Karelynne Ayayo. *Hermeneutics: Principles and Processes of Biblical Interpretation*. Grand Rapids, Mich.: Baker Academic, 2007.

Wal, Gijsbert van der. "Nieuwe generatie museumbezoekers vanmiddag in het," November 27, 2014, 3:44pm. Tweet. https://twitter.com/wijdopenogen/status/538085905987567616.

Weaver, Richard. *Ideas Have Consequences*. Chicago: University of Chicago Press, 1994.

"Westminster Shorter Catechism," *Center for Reformed Theology and Apologetics*. http://www.reformed.org/documents/WSC.html. Accessed May 25, 2017. Internet.

White, David F. *Practicing Discernment with Youth: A Transformative Youth Ministry Approach*. Youth Ministry Alternatives. Cleveland: Pilgrim, 2005.

Whitney, Donald S. *Family Worship*. Wheaton, Ill.: Crossway, 2016.

———. *Spiritual Disciplines for the Christian Life*. Colorado Springs: NavPress, 1991.

Wong, Kenman, and Scott Rae. *Business for the Common Good: A Christian Vision for the Marketplace*. Christian Worldview Integration Series. Downers Grove, Ill.: IVP, 2011.

Wright, Christopher. *The Mission of God's People: A Biblical Theology of the Church's Mission*. Biblical Theology for Life. Grand Rapids, Mich.: Zondervan, 2010.

Yaconelli, Mark. *Contemplative Youth Ministry: Practicing the Presence of Jesus*. Grand Rapids, Mich.: Zondervan/Youth Specialties, 2006.

"Youth Ministry and Youth Culture," *White Horse Inn Podcast*, June 22, 2014. https://www.white horseinn.org/2014/06/whi-1211-youth-ministry-youth-culture/ Accessed January 17, 2017. Internet.

Zacharias, Ravi. *The End of Reason: A Response to the New Atheists*. Grand Rapids, Mich.: Zondervan, 2008.

Zirschky, Andrew. *Beyond the Screen: Youth Ministry for the Connected But Alone Generation*. Nashville: Abingdon, 2015.

ACKNOWLEDGEMENTS

Writing this book has been full of drastic ebb and flow. Amidst the waves of excitement, as well as of frustration and even discouragement, I hope that the result is a helpful volume on youth and family ministry. I'm thankful for the kind words from friends, family, and students during this tumultuous process. Your words, whether they were a brief pick-me-up or a more serious pep talk, have helped me tremendously; thank you for practicing the truth of 1 Thessalonians 5:11.

I'd like to extend a specific thanks to those involved with Welch College Press. To Matt Bracey, thank you for your constant encouragement and keen eye as we walked through the editing process together. I appreciate your dedication and commitment to the Kingdom. To President J. Matthew Pinson, thank you for your years of mentorship and guidance as you've helped me to think through my philosophy of ministry.

To Frank Thornsbury, thank you for your love of the English language and for your commitment to making my use of it better. Lastly, to Jesse Owens, thanks for being a constant sounding board for creative ideas, as well as an encouraging friend.

To the men who provided the "Remodeling Tips," I thank God for your ministries. You are those whom I seek to imitate (1 Corinthians 11:1; 2 Thessalonians 3:7; Hebrews 13:7). You're in the thick of it as you work to be messengers of reconciliation (2 Corinthians 5:11-21) to this changing and diverse generation. Thank you for being committed to the gospel and to God's glory.

I also owe a debt of gratitude to my first youth leader, Mrs. Lynn Isaacs. She exemplified truth when I needed it the most: She taught me that unlovable people need love the most. She taught me always to care for the most marginalized. She first gave me an opportunity to minister, which has remained as a fire shut up in my bones (Jeremiah 20:9). Much of what I practice and teach in youth ministry has its roots in her example.

I'm also thankful to those who have helped shape my views of youth ministry. To Terry Forrest, Barry Raper, and Matthew McAffee, thank you for sitting with me and teaching me thoughtfully on how to minister to this current culture. I'm also thankful to Brian Cosby, Thomas Bergler, Alvin Reid, and Mark DeVries, whose writings about ministering to students have shaped my thoughts significantly.

I'm thankful to my God, who sent His Son Jesus Christ to pay the penalty for my sin and, upon faith in Christ, has sent His Holy Spirit to empower and to comfort. To Him alone be the glory now and forever. My life would be nothing and perishing without my God.

Lastly, I thank my wife, Rebekah. You have taught me grace and love in a way I never could have fathomed. You've been a constant encouragement. Thank you for always being the first eyes on anything that I write. Thank you for always seeing more potential in me than I see in myself. I love you.

ABOUT THE AUTHOR

Christopher Talbot serves as the Youth and Family Ministry Program Coordinator and Campus Pastor at Welch College, where he also teaches courses in biblical and theological studies. He holds degrees from Welch College (B.S.) and Grace College (M.A.), and he serves as Pastor of Youth and Family at Sylvan Park Free Will Baptist Church. Chris has spoken and written widely on youth and family ministry. He serves as Assistant Managing Editor for the *D6 Family Ministry Journal* and as a contributor for the Helwys Society Forum (thehsf.com). He is also a writer for the youth ministry website *Rooted* (rootedministry.com). Chris and his wife Rebekah live with their two sons in Gallatin, Tennessee.